Tales of the Modern World

essays

Gregg Fairbanks

Copyright © 2011 by Gregg Fairbanks

All rights reserved. No part of this book may be reproduced or transmitted in any form or by any means, electronic or mechanical, including photocopying, recording, or any information storage and retrieval system, without permission in writing from the Author.

ISBN 978-0-9837524-2-4

Table of Contents

Escape from Mediterranean Europe
    1. Castles in Spain   7
    2. Vamoose   10
    3. A Yankee in Yorkshire   18
    4. The Costa del Sol   23
    5. Palimpsest   28

London Jottings
    6. A View from a Garret   35
    7. Out and About   41
    8. Public Life   45
    9. Only the Queen Can Eat Swans   48

Overview
    10. Leaf Peeping   55
    11. Obsolescence   59
    12. Furniture   63
    13. What Happened to Christmas?   67
    14. Reading   70
    15. Copenhagen   73
    16. A New Decade   78
    17. Wake Up and Smell the Instant Coffee   82
    18. Castles and Cathedrals   85
    19. American Chop Suey   88
    20. Buying Food   90
    21. A Month in Beachwood Canyon   95
    22. Ketchup on White Bread   100
    23. The Sandwich Revisited   102
    24. Via Media   108
    25. Plating Food   111
    26. European Cucumbers   115
    27. Ball Games   118
    28. Fukushima Fallout   121

29. Mothers and Mockingbirds   124
30. Glimpses of a Child's World   129
31. The Crisis of Individual and System   134
32. The Dehumanization of Technology   136
33. Plan B   140

Escape from Mediterranean Europe

1
Castles in Spain

"People of Jimena—watch out! Foreign speculators are buying up your town." I shouted this, in Spanish, through a megaphone. I was standing on one side of the *Plaza Gibraltar*, the small square in the neighborhood where I was living in Spain. I had just done a rendition of the Beach Boys song "California Girls," that would have had Brian Wilson cringing. A group of young Spaniards loved the spectacle—or so they said. The scene was recorded on a mobile-phone video camera. Singing in public is a virtue in Andalusia. One of the group put me onto his shoulders and walked around the square—in the manner that bullfighters are carried out of the arena, after an impressive bullfight. After I had dismounted, six of them tossed me up into the air a few times. I was supine and airborne. As soon as I started grumbling, the town drew me in again. The Spanish could see the discontentment on my face, and they supported me with reinforcing gestures. There was a community there—people spoke to each other. *Jimenatos* often asked me encouragingly, if I was going to stay living in Jimena forever—as if that place were the land of Cockaigne. Nine years before coming to Spain, I left a place that I loved: Oia, Santorini. I was a prisoner of the place that I loved. When I was away from Oia, I longed to return. During the nine years that I lived there, the progress of the world affected a transformation in the village. It was turned into a tourist resort: a sanitized theme park in the Aegean Sea. I saw the handwriting on the wall. Conditions were deteriorating. The moment of decision occurred. I knew that it was time to go.

In 2002 I came to Jimena de la Frontera, in Andalusia. Somehow, I got stuck there. One day in 2008, I saw a tableau of abandoned junk at the end of my street. The *calle sin salida* sign, which had stood deceptively at the end of the street, had been uprooted and placed on its side, against the wall of an uninhabited building. In front of the sign there was a discarded wheel and tire from an old Renault automobile. Some metallic-blue paint had been haphazardly sprayed on it. Next to the wheel, there was a red-white-and-blue motorcycle. It was covered in black, greasy cobwebs and looked as though it had been dropped a few too many times to be rideable. The vinyl-covered, foam seat was rat-eaten. The dead-end sign was implanted at the beginning of the street when construction began, to connect it at the other end. At that time, the inhabitants of the street believed that the roadwork was for a pedestrian pathway. The misleading sign remained in place for months after the street had become a thoroughfare.

Returning home one night, crossing the *Plaza Gibraltar*, I was again given a ride on the shoulders of one of the adolescents who were in the habit of hanging around this square. They were congratulating me about something. Another one of them, who occasionally exhibited signs of a frontal-lobe dysfunction, took me onto his shoulders and proceeded to toss me onto the top of a parked car. The roof of the new Peugeot 307 crumpled a little, under my weight. I was happy to see that the sheet metal rebounded after I jumped down to the street. I decided to go to a tapa bar, for a drink. The owner of the bar was preparing some tapas. He was kneeling on the floor, hacking a chicken to bits, using an ax. The boney morsels were placed into a plastic container. Two customers, who were workers at a nearby stainless steel factory, were drinking coffee before leaving for work. The factory has some radioactive materials stored there. The exact nature of this waste is not public knowledge. It is rumored that the radioactive waste is a stockpile of contaminated fuel rods from nuclear power plants. The factory is located near to a petroleum refinery that was built by Spain's former dictator, Francisco Franco. The pollution-spewing eyesore is situated just to the east of Gibraltar, that last vestige of the British Empire. The area is usually enveloped in a pall of brown air. The region around the refinery has the highest cancer rate in Spain. Franco chose this location because it is upwind of Gibraltar. His intention was to drive away the Gibraltarians. They are still there, and the wind sometimes blows in the direction of Jimena.

The occasion was the opening celebration of a Mexican restaurant in Andalusia. Rather incongruously, I broke one thousand plates (with some assistance) in the street in front of the restaurant. Broken crockery was piled up a foot deep. Some drivers complained as they drove over the broken plates. Police cars occasionally drove up and stopped briefly at the periphery of the event. At the beginning of the inauguration, I was handed a plate and told to wait for the signal. When I got the signal, I smashed the plate. Then, the proprietress said, "*Now,* we're going to break one thousand more plates." Restaurant workers emerged from the restaurant, carrying piles of plates.

The Gypsy king, the titular leader of the clan in town, sat in the middle of the corner bar on the *Plaza de la Constitución,* facing out the door. He wore a wide-brimmed black hat. I walked down the street, carrying a toy machine gun that I had just purchased from a Chinese shop. It had flashing lights, made gunfire sounds, and had a little man on top, who was holding onto a second gun barrel. I walked into the doorway of the bar, aimed the gun at the Gypsy king, and pulled the trigger. Both barrels fired. The little man repeatedly screamed, "drop the gun." I then did an about-face, walked out of the bar, and sprayed some more noise inside the door.

Finally, the fat lady had sung. After six years of living in Jimena de la Frontera, I left town—leaving the expatriates who lived there, to pursue their dystopian dreams. I had had enough.

2
Vamoose

The security guard at the Gibraltar airport eyed me suspiciously. My carry-on case had just passed through the X-ray machine. He asked me: "Do you have any knives in this case?" My friend from Yorkshire, who was traveling with me, bolted to the airport bar that was next to the departure gates. He knows me and airport security and always goes through first.

"Only spoons," I replied, knowingly. "Heirlooms."

It was 2009, and I was on my way to Yorkshire, England. From 1984 to 1994 I lived in Greece. After returning to the United States, I had a persistent urge to recapture the experience of the way of life in Mediterranean Europe. In 2002 I came to live in Andalusia. The first years in Spain were interesting, but I began to find myself stuck in a kind of cultural abyss. Practical actions, which ought to require minutes, could takes days to accomplish. Crudely-built houses, unpalatable cuisine, and a way of life that, for too many, revolved around intoxication (cocaine and alcohol) and wasting time, made Andalusia a dismal place to live. Flamenco, the emblematic music of Andalusia, glorifies alcoholism, cocaine addiction, and self-destructive behavior. Expatriates who are inclined to swirl down the drain find Andalusia to be an ideal place to live. The disagreeable environment had the effect of retarding creative activity and forward movement. As I stood beside the gateway to the Mediterranean Sea, I was reminded of the impulse that had led me to my condition of progressively intensifying malaise. So much for the romance of Andalusia. I was leaving Spain.

The security guard proceeded to open my case and inspect its contents: books, papers, personal remembrances, and a plastic bag full of antique silver spoons. Another guard came over and stood beside his colleague. The plastic bag was opened, and the silverware was pulled out. There were spoons; a couple of serving forks; a fragile, nineteenth-century pie server; a mechanical pencil; and a small, silver pocketknife. There was also a sterling-silver baby rattle—in the shape of a pocket watch.

"What's this?" he asked me. He shook the rattle. "What's inside?"

"It was my baby rattle," I answered. "I don't know what's inside? It's been in there since before I was born."

The guard then held up the knife and waggled it in the air. He distorted his mouth into a mock smile and tilted his head to one side.

"Oh," I said. "I forgot about that. I thought there were just spoons in there."

"Spoons are okay," he assured me, just before he tossed the dangerous, *sharp* objects into a trash container that was directly behind him. I watched the forks, the mechanical pencil, the knife, and the pie server disappear. He proceed to flip through the books, carefully scrutinizing the bookmarks. A sharpened, wooden pencil was left where it was. A pencil sharpener wasn't taken away. He removed a handmade, rosewood doorknob from its bubble-wrapping and asked me if it was a gearshift knob. I said that it could be. Next, he opened a small canvas pouch that contained two silicon-bronze, violin-maker's finger-planes—with sharpened blades in place. I had completely forgotten that they were in the case. I wasn't overly concerned about the loss of the serving forks, but I didn't want to lose those planes. He examined the planes and then looked at me. He shook his head and placed them back into their pouch. He carefully repacked the case and let me go on my way. I glanced at the trash bin and then hurried to the bar—for a pint of beer.

Four months earlier, when I was flying on this same route, I was handed an orange-colored, paper pouch: a gift for the passengers on the airline's inaugural flight on that route. The package contained a *glass* ornament—in the shape of the Rock of Gibraltar.

Before leaving Spain, I was told that I had to get an NIE number in order to pay my medical insurance. My insurance premium was automatically withdrawn from a bank account that I had set up for that exclusive purpose. The account had been frozen by the bank. A new Spanish law required me to have an NIE number in order to have a bank account. I had had the account for several years, but suddenly I couldn't deposit or withdraw money until I obtained this number from the *Policía Nacional*. On one of my last days in Spain, I left my house, to take care of this business. Five hours later, after a taxi ride, a train ride, and a bus ride, I arrived in La Linea, the Spanish town next to Gibraltar. After walking across the town, I arrived at the headquarters of the National Police. The policeman in the office that dealt with papers for foreigners had a reputation for being a fascist xenophobe. When my turn came, I sat down in front of his desk and handed him my papers. I had a permanent visa for Spain. He glanced at my official documentation and then tossed them across the desk.

"*No vale nada!*" (These are worth nothing!) "*Muchos Americanos,*" he said, with a sarcastic and disgusted tone in his voice. He then flatly refused to give me an NIE number—I had no right to have one, he said. He picked up my passport and stared at it, leafing through it slowly, page by excruciating page. He stopped on one page and glared at it intently. He exhibited some evident satisfaction. He went back to reexamine some other pages before returning to the one that interested him the most. Another good, long stare.

He handed me my passport and said, "You have four days to leave Spain. Your time has almost expired." This judgement was based on my return to Spain, from a trip to America, the previous October. Despite my permanent visa, he insisted that I was allowed to stay in Spain for only three months: the time allowed for tourists from the United States.

"I'm leaving in five days," I replied politely—before leaving, to go forward on the second half of my ten-hour errand. I later learned that I actually needed an NIA number, but no one was capable of telling me that.

When I arrived in Yorkshire, I quickly learned that, when stepping off the curb into the street, I had to consciously develop the habit of looking to the right. My brain has been conditioned from childhood, to look left. It is said that driving on the left-hand side of the road comes from the tradition of having one's sword-arm next to the oncoming lane. In days of yore, left-handed people were at a disadvantage.

Yorkshire is a distinct cultural region in England. It is the largest county in England. It consists of four parts: West Yorkshire, East Yorkshire, South Yorkshire, and North Yorkshire. The people there identify themselves as being from Yorkshire. The houses are solidly-built, from brick and stone. (I couldn't help thinking about the story of *The Three Little Pigs*.) Milkmen still deliver glass bottles of milk and cream to the back steps of houses. This practice disappeared in my life in America, about 1960. In England there is a curious propensity for queasy patterns on carpets and upholstery. There was a disconcerting presence of nervous men in cheap black suits, who walked about in the midst of the others, usually with miserable looks on their faces. They were white-collar workers. I could never get to the bottom of why their color of choice was black. Most people in Yorkshire reserve their black suits for funerals. There are large numbers of Pakistanis living in Yorkshire, many of whom walk around dressed in the customary garb of their native land. Many women wear burkas. There is resentment in Yorkshire. Many of the heroin dealers in that part of England are Pakistani. I shudder to think about the number of slices of boiled ham that have been imbedded in the mortar, behind tiles in mosques in Yorkshire.

There were Chinamen wandering about in Yorkshire. They came up to me in pubs, at the oddest moments, to sell me bootleg DVDs of recently released films. Some of these were copies of the official DVDs that are sent to individuals who vote for the Oscars. Other DVDs had a Russian connection.

In England there is a ubiquitous presence of closed-circuit television cameras. Lenses peer down from the tops of poles on virtually every street. These CCTV surveillance cameras are installed on buses and trains. They are mounted outside of pubs and, in some cases, inside of pubs. The are present in nearly every public place. Mobile CCTVs are mounted in trucks, which cruise around, trying to detect antisocial behavior. There is a cheerful post-Orwellian ambience in Yorkshire. Nobody takes much notice of the cameras. People *are* annoyed by the complex obstructions of red tape: the bureaucratic regulations that snarl up their lives. Most people in Yorkshire are friendly and direct. There is a rich use of the English language. The Yorkshire dialect is spoken with a strong accent. The meanings of many words that originated in Yorkshire have been bent in the American translation. The humor in Yorkshire is substantial and deep-rooted. People have a *sense* of humor. Repartee is challenging. Avoid using *the Boston Tea Party* as a conversational icebreaker. People in Yorkshire are inclined to smile.

The town markets in Yorkshire have stalls selling wide varieties of things. There are butchers, fishmongers, bakers, greengrocers, and cheese vendors. There are also stalls selling clothing, shoes, fishing tackle, candy, stationery, toys, pet supplies, cosmetics, and varieties of miscellaneous household goods and what have you. In villages there are small shops—the kind that are becoming outmoded in small American towns, due to the big-box phenomenon. In towns in England, modern shopping malls stand alongside the traditional markets.

And, of course, there are pubs—everywhere: stations of public life, places to meet people and have a talk. There are many varieties of bitters, ales, and lagers. A curious note: the condom machines, in some pubs in Yorkshire, dispense inflatable sheep.

There is a commonly-held myth that the cuisine in England consists mainly of fish-and-chips and assorted stodges, such as bangers-and-mash, mushy peas, bubble-and-squeak, cottage pie, and shepherd's pie. These simple meals are the deceptive tip of a culinary iceberg. The cuisine of Yorkshire is full of delectable surprises. The foodstuffs available are remarkable in quality and variety. The meats, fresh seafood, and produce are delicious. There are extraordinary cheeses (the Wensleydales are exquisite) and peculiar relishes, such as piccalilli and ploughman's pickle. There are wide varieties of baked goods: savory pies and pasties (hand-held pies), sweet tarts (custard, treacle, Yorkshire curd, apple, apple-and-blackberry, among others), scones, cakes, and other pastries. And there is no shortage of Yorkshire pudding.

There is an ample diversity of foods available for eating on the hoof. I tended to avoid the shops that seemed to have been designed to cater primarily to drunken lager-louts. One night, in one of these establishments, I ordered a "doner kebab." I was handed a cardboard container that held a heap of cheap salad, mixed with slices of meat that had been cut from a vertical spit—all piled atop a limp, gratuitous, pita-like membrane. I immediately gave up the thought of eating this concoction as a sandwich. The price added insult to injury. I thought about the *giros* I had eaten in Greece: thick, crispy, toasted pita bread, turned into a cone-shape and filled with succulent meat, ripe tomatoes, garlicky *tzatziki,* and sliced onion—delicious and very handy to eat. I scarfed down as much of this melange as I could, using the plastic fork provided, while I pondered the concept of user-friendly street food—before I tossed the residua into a trash bin. In England there is a seventy-five pound fine for littering. The only appreciable gastronomic sensation had been the spiciness of the meat. I suspect that I had not drunk enough beer to appreciate the experience properly.

I *have* eaten many delicious snacks while walking around in Yorkshire. At a market stall that sold seafood, I ate fresh whelks and cockles (sprinkled with malt vinegar, dusted with salt and pepper, and sold in paper cups). I frequently found myself munching on hot, meat-filled pasties, purchased from shops that are everywhere. One national chain of pasty shops sports my first name as its own. Coming out of one of these shops, my first week in Yorkshire, I heard someone exclaim in amazement, "There are *Greggs,* fucking *everywhere!*" On one of my first days in Yorkshire, not paying sufficient attention in a fish-and-chips shop, I inadvertently ordered a *chip butty:* fried potatoes sandwiched in a roll. I was forced to acquire a taste for brown sauce, the ketchup of England.

One afternoon, in Sheffield, I purchased an ostrich burger, from a tent that was set up on a pedestrian walkway. I garnished it with a sweet chilli sauce (they spell chili with two *L*s in England). A few minutes later, I was sipping a pint of bitter in a pub. The ostrich burger was delicious, but it had left an aftertaste, which was interfering with my enjoyment of the beer. I sucked down the pint and walked off to find a pastry shop. I proceeded to cleanse my palate, with a Yorkshire curd tart. I then went to another pub, to enjoy a pint.

I was away from home one Saturday night, having a few pints in another town. It became too late to return home on the trains. My friend saw his nephew, in the pub that we were in. We arranged to sleep at his house. My friend insisted that I write down the address in my notebook. His nephew balked at giving it to me, saying that we would all leave together. A few minutes later, he disappeared. An hour after that discovery, we got a taxi and gave the driver the address. My friend's nephew wasn't answering his mobile phone or responding to his doorbell. Numerous attempts were made. My friend began pounding on the front door. At that point I decided to check the address in the notebook, just to be sure it was the right house. A grey-bearded Pakistani man came out of the front door of the next house, to smoke a cigarette, while he scrutinized us. After we explained our circumstances to him, he was able to confirm that it was the nephew's house. A description sufficed. The neighbor seemed to be relieved and went back inside. Next, my friend went around to the side of the house and jumped over the gate, into the fenced-in backyard. He picked up a metal pole that was intended to be used to prop up the clothesline and began to try to pry open the kitchen window. I stood on the other side of the fence, on the sidewalk. A helicopter flew over. A minute later, two police cars came down the street. One parked directly in front of me; the other one parked about ten yards ahead. When I saw them coming down the street, I said to my friend: "You'd better stop now. The cops are here."

He jumped over the fence, rather than over the metal gate. This turned out to be a mistake because, attached to the top of the fence, there were strips of wood that had rows of nails projecting upward from them—the things that are used to install wall-to-wall carpet. My friend immediately looked at his hands. There was a row of nail punctures on both palms. He asked one of the policemen, if it was legal to have that sort of thing on the top of a fence—before he explained that he was trying to break into the house. Our names were put through a hand-held computer. We turned up clean. They never checked our identification. When a policewoman asked me how I spelled my first name, I replied: "Like the pasty shops."

I explained what had been going on—the truth of it. And finally, in order to clearly make the point, I turned to a male policeman (so as not to be disrespectful to the woman to whom I was telling the story) and said: "The thing is this—his nephew, cousin, or whatever he is, is a ?!%§!"

After being advised to find someplace else to sleep for the night, we walked off, down the street. As we approached the main road, to find a taxi to take us to a hotel, the policewoman yelled: "Hey! Come back guys. You're *in*." My friend's nephew had decided to answer his mobile phone when the police began ringing his number. He had been watching the whole event, through his bedroom window. It was a good thing that it was the right house.

I have to admit that, in Yorkshire, I often have crumpets and tea, the first thing in the morning.

3
A Yankee in Yorkshire

The first thing that I want to say is that people in Yorkshire think that they want to eat fried potatoes ("chips," they are called in England) with pizza. The chips usually don't get eaten, but they are there, like a greasy centerpiece on the table. What is it, with fried potatoes in England? In Yorkshire they want to eat them with everything. The *chip butty* is the most baffling thing: fried potatoes sandwiched in a bun. I felt obliged to refer to these as "starch sandwiches." And, the one and only time that I made the mistake of ordering one—in a fish-and-chips shop—they had no ketchup. Either that or I was too shocked to inquire about it. As they say in Yorkshire: at the end of the day, it's all good fun—except for the occasional indigestion.

Crossing the road can be dangerous in Yorkshire. Not only because the cars are all going in the wrong direction, but because drivers refuse to slow down for pedestrians. Not only do they not brake, they don't even take their foot off the accelerator—and some of the drivers might have just left a pub.

In England it is necessary to have a license in order to watch TV. Failure to have such a license can result in a one thousand pound fine. There are vans equipped with TV detection gizmos, that are used to catch people in the act. These vans prowl around the streets, trying to find offenders. The drivers can legally enter your house, to inspect it. The eerie feeling of waiting for the unexpected knock-knock at your door. When you move into a new place, warnings come in the mail, almost daily. Your mailbox gets so jammed with these threats, that there is no room for the other mail. Every threatening postcard has a different telephone number to call. I tried to call a few of these numbers, just for fun. None of them connected to anything. It's unnerving when these vans park directly in front of your house, just waiting for someone to turn on the unlicensed television. Sometimes, the detection vans park in front for a while and then go away—or so they would like you to believe. Take a quick walk around the block, and you see them parked just out of sight of your windows, around a corner. I don't even like TV.

One morning, I tossed the TV into the trash bin that was behind the apartment. But not without quickly looking around, to see if there were any of the TV gestapo lurking in the parking lot. A couple of days later, I saw the detection truck, once again parked across the street. I was watching the BBC news, on the Internet. They can't get you for that—the license is only required for broadcast transmissions. There was a moment when I thought to revert to my youthful enthusiasm and go to the window and give the man in the van, the finger—but I thought better of it.

The place where I lived is an economically depressed area. It was a region of coal miners. The Industrial Revolution took place in that region of England. After the coal-miner's strike in the 1980s, Margaret Thatcher closed the coal mines. The results are still being felt. In the area where I lived, the coal miners had been "hard-liners."

I lived in a white-collar, black-suit housing development that was on the edge of a village. I would have preferred to live in an old brick house, but the pressures of time led me to that abode. The housing development was built on top of a coal pit. I couldn't imagine how anyone could be fool enough to buy one of those houses. The plaster was already cracking in the house, and it was new. Walking around these houses reminded me of walking around suburbia in America. Few people were inclined to greet you. I had to go to the pub every day, where people spoke to me.

There is a curious fashion among some of the male youths in England. They wear baggy blue jeans, halfway down their behinds. Their intention is to expose the back side of their underpants. There was a lot of designer underwear in evidence. The older men in Yorkshire, just shook their heads and rolled their eyes.

On Mondays I went to the Barnsley Market. It was a five-minute train ride down the line. Darton, the village where I lived, is a part of the municipality of Barnsley. The plate-glass shops in that town had a good business. On weekends, drunken lager-louts, high on beer and white powders, would routinely smash windows in Barnsley.

I once made a train change in Wakefield, late on a Saturday night. There are two train stations in Wakefield. I had to walk from one train station, to the other. While I was walking to the next station, I had an experience that was like a scene from a David Lynch movie. I stood there on a sidewalk, chomping on a doner kebab, with my mouth gaping open. A drunk passed by and commented on my rude way of chewing food. Tarted-up blond women (hundreds of them, not all of whom were naturally blond), who were wearing the most miniscule clothing possible (and it was winter), were swarming everywhere.

One of the problems with many pubs is that you can't, except at odd moments, get any food—except peanuts and potato chips (which are called "crisps," in England). The crisps are quite often laced with monosodium glutamate. There was also cocaine, ketamine, and some kind of plant fertilizer floating about and going up people's noses. WD-40 was sprayed on windowsills in pub toilets, to discourage the laying down of lines of white powders. I had a local pub which was cozy. As I said, I had to go every day. I drank John Smith's bitter.

On a couple of occasions, I went to pubs in Sowerby Bridge, in West Yorkshire. My family left that town in 1633. They settled in America. Each time I went to Sowerby Bridge, I mentioned my surname and was welcomed by the locals. On my way home from Sowerby Bridge, I always managed to catch the last train out of Leeds, on my way back to Darton. When people joked to me about my family leaving Yorkshire, I often replied that my family got out when the going was good. But, I never said that in Sowerby Bridge.

One sunny Sunday afternoon, I decided to walk to a pub that was a couple of villages away. I was looking forward to eating some food and drinking a few pints of beer. After a bracing walk down roads brimming with BMWs, I arrived at the pub. I was thirsty. The inside of the pub was beautiful. There were wooden beams everywhere. I ordered a pint of bitter and a plate of pâté and toast. The toast was toasted just enough to make the bread stale. Its whiteness was an obvious indication of its under-toasted condition. I complained about the condition of the toast. The bartender told me that they had a new cook. It was his first day. I told the bartender that I learned to make toast before I could read. The pâté was okay. Later, I ordered a plate of nachos. A plate of nachos was served to me: a pile of tortilla chips (sub-mediocre quality), with a large glob of cheese melted on the summit of the user-unfriendly concoction. There had been no attempt to distribute the cheese. And, there was an inadequate quantity of guacamole. But, the antique, wooden roof structure in the pub was very aesthetically pleasing. The number of pubs in England is diminishing. People cite as causes: smoking bans, increased beer taxes, and the current economic crisis. As one pub pundit put it: "Some of them are just crap." When the bartender got off work, he drove me to a pub that was located next to a canal. A couple of hours later, I wanted to buy a narrowboat and toss in my gear. People live on these narrowboats, which are fully self-contained, albeit narrow, floating houses that cruise along the extensive canal network in England. The canals were built during the Industrial Revolution. This dream still lingers in my mind. Later that night, the Pakistani taxi driver who took me home wanted to discuss God. I said that there was probably only one. He told me that I was a good person. I gave him a tip.

    One of the best pubs in Yorkshire is the pub that is located inside the train station in Dewsbury. A door connects the pub to the train platform. This pub serves delicious sandwiches and has hand-pulled ales—a large selection. The pub sells T-shirts that have imprinted on them: "*I missed the train at Dewsbury*." I frequently did and on one occasion bought a T-shirt. There is a coal fireplace at one end of the pub—very cozy on winter afternoons. One of the regular customers in this pub kept telling me that there was another American living in Yorkshire, who looked just like me. He had encountered this American in various places in Yorkshire. I had heard this on several occasions before it finally dawned on me: *I* was the other American in Yorkshire.

Occasionally, someone would tell me that Clint Eastwood is Stan Laurel's son. Stan Laurel was born in Cumbria, the county to the north of Yorkshire, where Sellafield, one of the world's nuclear dustbins, is located. Clint Eastwood's father was a steel worker in San Francisco. I was waiting for them to tell me that Oliver Hardy was Rush Limbaugh's father. But perhaps, in Yorkshire, they had never heard of Rush. Flapping your necktie is one thing. Flapping the American flag is quite another thing.

In 1911 Harry Houdini was padlocked inside a metal cask of Tetley's ale. This event took place at the Tetley's brewery in Leeds, in Yorkshire. Houdini was an escapologist, but he couldn't get out. He had to be released. I know how he felt. I hope that he liked it in there as much as I did.

4
The Costa del Sol
(the land of lemmings and crooks)

After six months of living in Yorkshire, England, I found myself returning to Andalusia—to a new place. I had little recourse. I had been given a six-month stamp in my passport—the maximum that a tourist can stay in England. England is not part of the Schengen Area. The Schengen Area includes most of the European Union and a few other countries that are not a part of the EU. The Schengen Area functions as a single state, for purposes of travel. Tourists are allowed a maximum stay of three months. After three months, tourists must remain outside of the Schengen Area for three months before being allowed to return for three more months. Americans are not allowed to live in the Schengen Area, without a visa. I had a permanent Schengen visa, for living in Spain. It was my slippery foothold in Europe. It existed as long as I maintained a residence in Spain.

After arriving at the Gibraltar airport, I had lunch at a small restaurant in "Gib," before I proceeded to a hotel in the town where I was to live, which is near to Marbella, on the Costa del Sol. Somehow, a Spanish woman ended up sitting at my table. She worked for an Internet gambling company that is based in Gibraltar. The owner of the company, a multimillionaire, was from India, and he didn't eat beef. On a recent trip to Paris, he chose to have his lunch in a Burger King. He ate a meatless Whopper. For some reason, this Andalusian woman felt impelled to explain to me that Andalusians don't like to work. "We just like to relax and enjoy ourselves," she informed me. I was familiar with the fiesta-siesta cycle in Andalusia. The manifest results of this cultural impulse are quite evident there.

I said, "I am an artist, and I enjoy my work."

She seemed perplexed. "Oh! It's a hobby," she concluded.

"No. I've been doing this since I was twenty years old. It's not a hobby," I told her. I'm not sure that she got the point.

At first glance, the Costa del Sol resembles a sloppily-done imitation of southern California or Arizona, liberally sprinkled with golf courses. The coastline is a sprawling concrete conurbation, which extends from the vulgarian opulence of the mansions of Sotogrande, to just beyond the city of Malaga. Kitschy-looking, slapped-together apartment blocks and strip malls stretch along the coastal region. Shoddy construction and aesthetically-crude design are typical. In the 1980s a well-known travel guide removed the Costa del Sol from its Spanish guidebook because they didn't consider it to be, strictly speaking, a part of Spain. Thirty years ago, Marbella was a chic jet-set destination. Bob Hope used to go there. There is still some residua of jet-set culture there: pockets of high-end real estate. But the scene has faded. The waned chic has overtones of an old whore trying to hang on to her youthful beauty. The quality of the restaurants ranges from dubious to wretched.

Shortly after I arrived on the Costa del Sol, a five-million-euro mansion washed down a cliff, after some heavy rains. Perhaps the owner should have hired a competent architect before he built it. Tests of soil conditions might have been appropriate. There is little evidence of the existence of competent architects on the Costa del Sol. Construction in that region has virtually come to a standstill. Many illegally built hotels and apartment blocks are to be torn down. Much of the real estate development was financed through money laundering. Mafias and people engaged in fraud find the Costa del Sol to be an ideal base of operations. Political corruption is the norm.

A local newspaper reported that one of the beaches on the Costa del Sol was rated as being one of the top ten most beautiful beaches in the world. I have seen this beach, and it is one of the ugliest beaches that I have ever seen. You couldn't pay me to sit on it. I *have* seen beautiful beaches—on the coast of California; in France—on the Côte d'Azur and on the coast of Brittany; in the Scottish Highlands; on Greek islands; on the coast of Maine;

on the coast of Rhode Island; and on Cape Cod, in Massachusetts. Newspapers on the Costa del Sol are full of self-congratulatory drivel.

I heard about a Dane who had been living on the Costa del Sol. He moved from the coast, to a little town in the hills, which is renowned for being full of cocaine addicts and alcoholics. He rented a house that is directly across the road from the entrance to the town dump. He claimed to be delighted with his new abode. Perhaps he liked the smell of burning plastic wafting into his house.

There are various groups of expatriates who have come to live on the Costa del Sol, for "a life in the sun." The sociological hodgepodge on the Costa del Sol is composed of people from England, Ireland, Scotland, Denmark, Norway, Sweden, Finland, Holland, Russia, Italy, Morocco, Romania, Poland, China, and assorted South American countries—among others. There are also some Africans from Senegal, many of whom are the "lookie-lookie men." They wander through the streets, searching for tourists, in order to sell them sunglasses, cheap Rolex-like wristwatches, and colorful handbags and wallets that sport designer names. They also peddle DVDs of movies that have been recorded with camcorders in movie theaters. The Costa del Sol is something of a weed field of humanity.

The Costa del Sol is infested with assorted mafias. Thugs and goons move around in the shadows on the "Costa del Crime." Offices open and close, as enterprises engaged in frauds and swindles change their addresses. Porto Banus abounds with poseurs, wannabes, hangers-on, prostitutes, and tourists. Ferraris, Maseratis, and Lamborghinis can be seen plying the streets, in search of attention. There are a few yachts tied up in Puerto Banus. They form the backdrop for a lot of overpriced, third-rate bars and eateries. Fifty years ago, the place was a scant village, with dirt roads. All along the Costa del Sol, people hang around the fringe of the wealth, scurrying around, feeding off the scraps, hoping to extract a little of what flows out of the pockets of the rich. Drug and alcohol abuse lubricate the cultural system. Diogenes could wander around there all day, with his lamp, and come up empty. The culture resembles a predatory, parasitic organism that is consuming itself. Birds of a feather flock together—so they say.

The now not-so-deluxe Costa del Sol is fizzling out. The region is becoming a low-rent destination for package-holiday tourists. It is a bit passed its sell-by date. With the coming of the "crisis," the tourism economy began to deteriorate. One evening, I was in a bar, having a drink. Two young Irish women came into the bar, to enjoy their holiday. The bartender asked them why they had chosen that place for their vacation destination. They replied that it was one of the cheapest places that they had found on the Internet. One of the two then asked the bartender, if it was possible to get a taxi to Barcelona—they thought that they would like to have a look at it. The bartender replied that, probably, it was possible—but it was one thousand kilometers up the coast.

For ten years after Franco's death, in 1975, Spain engaged in an intoxicated fiesta, celebrating the demise of the dictator. In the mid 1980s the Spanish government decided that it had to crack down on this—a little. The Spanish appear to have carried on with this fiesta. Generalíssimo Francisco Franco is still dead!

Murphy must have written his famous law while he was in Andalusia. I have never seen any place, where it applied more. The developed coastal region known as the Costa del Sol is the result of one of Francisco Franco's experiments. It was originally conceived to be a tourist region within a fascist dictatorship. It turned out to be a Mecca for less-than-legal activities and for tourists who have bad taste in places. Money laundering financed a proliferation of shoddy, substandard housing construction on the Costa del Sol—leading to a real estate bubble. The bubble has popped. Expatriates are now trying to sell their devalued and leaking real estate. A few years earlier, they were flocking there from Britain and other northern European countries, lured by the promise of sunshine. Now, a reflux diaspora is beginning—back to rainy Britain and the cold regions of northern Europe.

My dream of living again in a culture in Mediterranean Europe led me to Andalusia. After living ten years on Greek islands, this impulse was implanted in my brain. When I allow myself a moment for some Monday morning quarterbacking, I wonder what I was thinking. This misguided divagation landed me in Andalusia. Why did the moron throw the alarm clock out the window? To see time fly? Maybe it was to try to kill time. Killing time seems to be a fundamental part of the Andalusian way of life. I think that the only thing that keeps Spanish women from tearing their hair out is the ubiquitous presence of hairstyling salons.

There were two televisions commercials in Spain, which baffled me. One of these, showed two men gleefully dumping cans of corn onto hamburgers. In the other ad, Heinz ketchup was being squirted onto a piece of fish. What can I say—that's not my cup of tea. After living eight years in Spain, I finally left. I made a rather abrupt departure.

5
Palimpsest
(Hell as Greece)

I decided to return to Greece. After eight years, I was finally leaving Spain, precariously on my way to Greece—farther into an abyss. My impulse to return to Mediterranean Europe couldn't have been more misguided. Twenty-five years ago, Greece was a paradise. Things have changed. I arrived in Greece in September. I hadn't been in Greece in more than sixteen years. I returned, to visit the village where I had lived, the last year of the ten years that I lived in Greece. When I left Greece, in March 1994, I had been pressured to leave the country, for some unknown reason, by the national security police. It was an impulsive move to return to Greece. I was curious about what was going on there, and I wanted, at any cost, to get out of Spain. The news media was showing only sound bites of politicians and images of the riots taking place in Athens. I wanted to see what was going on in the villages.

On my way to Greece, I passed through the Zurich airport. Going down the moving walkways, I expected to see a life-size picture of Nastassja Kinski, naked, with a python wrapped around her. Then, I realized that that poster had been there twenty-five years earlier, when I had lived in Greece before. Time flies. The poster had been replaced with an advertisement for a bank.

The old culture is evaporating in Greece. The Greeks were unprepared for the jolt into the global consumer society that they have undergone. In Athens, some people were eating out of trash containers. The almond trees surrounding the village where I stayed were left largely untouched. In groves around the village, oranges and lemons were left to fall on the ground. Mylar packages of wood-like almonds, produced somewhere in the EU, were sold in the village. People bought fruit that was shipped into the village from somewhere else.

I stayed in a Byzantine, pentagon-shaped fortress village, with narrow, labyrinthine passageways and a small central square. The church, which is on one side of the square, contains life-size icons of the archangels Gabriel and Michael. The atmosphere in the village was rather dismal. Prices in Greece were exorbitant. More and more crippling taxation was being imposed. People had been seduced into taking out bank loans. Everybody was in debt. People borrowed from one, to pay another. Many people had a tendency to not pay debts. Sometimes, businesses in Greece didn't pay employees. It was becoming a desolate culture. The village where I stayed had recently been declared to be a national monument. The architecture still remained. New codes that were imposed by archaeologists were hampering what little business was left in the village. Tourism was dwindling. The cost of things was absurdly high, in a country that was once a very inexpensive destination. Tourism accounts for a large part of the Greek economy. An inexpensive, charming, quaint, antique culture has been transformed into an expensive, miserable backwater of Europe. Years ago, people had come to experience an authentic culture. That culture is now disappearing. The freedom that had existed for foreigners and Greeks alike has disappeared. The days of making a business on a shoestring are over. Twenty-five years ago, the connection of the people to the governmental systems was minimal. Now, the bureaucracy is right in their faces. The euro was a time-release, economic neutron bomb dropped on the villages of Greece.

Greek pride in their culture has been cut down a few notches. Greece is one of the PIIGS: Portugal, Ireland, Italy, Greece, and Spain. These countries have had their economies decimated. This is partly due to endemic corruption. European Union funding went into the pockets of a few people at the top. The governments sold treasury bonds to finance the countries. Greece was the first to go down, then Ireland, and as I write this, Portugal has fallen. The European Union is borrowing money in order to loan it to the PIIGS, so that they can pay their debts. It is like a loans-and-debts shell game—a macroeconomic version of the microeconomic shell game that is being played in villages in Greece. Where is the money coming from? The Greeks blame their politicians and the bureaucracy of the European Union. They are clearly aware now, that the introduction of the euro led to the ruin of their country. After it came into use, prices skyrocketed in Greece. The "debt crisis" is reverberating in the eurozone.

Shortly before I left Greece, there was a festival in the village, celebrating Clean Monday: the beginning of Lent in the Eastern Orthodox Church. The village square was packed with people. Gold-laden and bejeweled Athenian wives strutted around in their gaudy attire. Food and drink were consumed. This celebration didn't have the atmosphere of the festivals that I had experienced in Greece, a quarter of a century earlier. It was rather perfunctory.

During the festival, I walked into a restaurant, to have something to eat. Someone at one of the tables beckoned to me and invited me to sit down and have some wine and food. I had never seen this person before. He began by asking me too many questions. He was more than just a curious Greek. He wrote down the name of my hometown and my name, and put the paper into his pocket. He proceeded to tell me that he was a sniper for the military. He told me that he had been in Kosovo during the Yugoslav Wars. At that time, Greece snuck some troops over the border—to fight on the wrong side of that war. He told me that his job was to kill people—when *they* told him to. At one point in the conversation, I asked him if he was planning on killing me. He said *no*, he had no such plans. "You're a nice guy," he said.

In Greece, the old ways are rapidly being abandoned. New ways have been only partly adopted. Progress is coming to a standstill—stunted by the economic debt crisis of the Greek government. The Greeks had one foot in the door before they slammed it on their own foot. The oldest generation in Greece is dying off. Old people floated around the village, like phantoms from another time. There was a funeral every couple of weeks. A dolorous ringing, coming from the church bell tower, announced the deaths. The generation of people in their twenties were neither here nor there. They didn't understand the modern world, and they didn't want to remember the old ways. And, there are few donkeys left, if gasoline were to become in short supply. The Greeks will experience some difficulty, reverting to former ways of life. They killed the goose that laid the golden eggs.

My mistaken pursuit of Mediterranean Europe led me to the dead end of a long blind alley. I was drowning in a dearth of cultural stimuli. It was rather anticlimactic. Two days before I was to become an illegal alien in the Schengen Area, I left Greece. I was headed for London. When I left Spain, my Spanish visa became effectively defunct. I had ninety days left before I had to exit the Schengen Area. (The Schengen Area includes most of the European Union and also Iceland, Switzerland, and Norway, which are not part of the EU.) The Schengen Agreement was implemented to control immigration. Europe is being overrun by Chinese, while the entry of Americans is strictly regulated. England and Ireland are not part of the Schengen Area, although they are part of the European Union.

At the passport control in Zurich, where I passed out of the Schengen Area, I handed my passport to the official, without the visa. I wanted to see what would happen. After scanning my passport into a computer, he proceeded to examine my passport. He went through it three times, looking for my most recent entry stamp. The most recent one was more than two years old. After a minute of his perusing my passport, I revealed the documentation of the last vestiges of my Spanish Schengen visa. He said that, in that case, he wouldn't give me an exit stamp. At the passport control in Heathrow Airport, in London, I was given a stamp that allowed me to stay in Britain for six months. I was facing a looming limbo. There are no retakes on the event horizon.

London Jottings

6
A View from a Garret

London Bridge is falling down,
Falling down, falling down.

I am now living in London—nominally speaking. I rent a room on the top floor of a house on the outskirts of that great city. The house is located on the fringe of a suburban shopping district in the southwestern quadrant of Greater London, in the county of Surrey. The town where I live is partly within the Royal Borough of Kingston-upon-Thames and partly within the London Borough of Merton. I live on the Merton side of the tracks. The conurbation that is Greater London comprises a rather large area. I know I must be in London—I see red, double-decker buses everywhere. My window overlooks a Krispy Kreme Doughnuts shop that is just down the block. It is occasionally a source of solace. Every Sunday morning, there is a parade of customized cars, hot rods, and antique cars passing below my window. The car enthusiasts use the Krispy Kreme parking lot as their meeting place.

The building I live in resembles what I imagine halfway houses for ex-cons look like. The top floors of a house have been converted into a rooming house. There are six rooms, with two shared baths and a shared kitchen. The entrance is through a back alley. When I moved into the house, I noticed that there were two plates of petrified food on the kitchen table. The kitchen resembles what I imagine kitchens look like in houses that are shown on Chernobyl sightseeing tours. Except for the street food that I eat on the run, I survive on bunker food and Nescafe: cold buffet on my desk. I use the kitchen, only to boil the water for my coffee. In other words, I graze.

On the side of the house where I live, just outside my window, there is a billboard which alternates between three advertisements. Louvers flop around, revealing the signs in sequence. When I moved in, the ads were for a mouthwash for bleeding gums, women's shoes, and frozen broccoli florets. C*lop—clop—clop*. It sounds like a horse's hoof stomping on cobblestones. The room that I rent is located on what appears to be a misplaced, disjoint fragment of some "High Street." On High Streets the ground floors of row houses have been converted into storefront businesses. Shops are typically plastered with gaudy signs. The ground floor of the building where I live houses a custom-kitchen showroom. The kitchens that are on display cause me to cringe—when I think of my own accommodations. Around the corner there is a giant supermarket. In my neighborhood there are a couple of minimarts, a lumber yard, a gigantic builder's supply, a tool rental shop, an automotive parts store, a showroom selling bathroom fixtures, and several restaurants—an Indian restaurant, a Pakistani restaurant, a Korean restaurant, and an Italian restaurant that has singers performing on a regular basis, doing tributes to Frank Sinatra and Rod Stewart. There is also a storefront containing the residual traces of the presence of a Chinese herbalist and acupuncturist that went out of business.

There is a slight dismalness to my neighborhood. A twenty minute bus ride takes me to the town center of Kingston-upon-Thames. Farther down the road, and another bus ride away, is Richmond-upon-Thames: an opulent upper-class town that looks like one imagines England ought to look like. Mick Jagger lives there—among others. On my way home from Kingston, I take the bus that is headed to Tooting Broadway.

"Oyster cards" are a vital part of life in London. They are plastic smartcards with which one pays bus fares, subway fares, and train fares, by touching the card onto an electronic reader. Oyster cards are an economic necessity. Paying cash results in significantly higher fares—nearly double. Bus fares are more than two dollars—almost four dollars, if paid at the point of entry. Putting credit on mobile phones and Internet dongles, and topping up Oyster cards is an integral part of daily life in London. Top-ups are lifelines to the world.

London is composed of thirty-two boroughs, plus the City of London: the central core of the city, which is slightly more than one square mile in size—the boundaries of which are more or less the same as they were in the Middle Ages. Twelve of the boroughs plus the City of London form Inner London. The other twenty boroughs compose Outer London. The City of London is about ten miles away from where I live—a bus ride, a train ride—then into the Tube. The London Underground is a baffling, labyrinthine subway system. A seemingly endless swarm of humanity courses through it every day. There is a subway stop named Goodge, which has elevators going down to the train platforms, which are deep below the city. This station was used as a bomb shelter during the blitzkrieg in World War II. The subway is called "the Tube" because the pedestrian passageways and the train tunnels are tube-shaped. The London Underground is the oldest underground railway in the world.

There is nothing particularly impressive about the London Bridge. Nor was there anything particularly impressive about the former, nineteenth-century London Bridge. Because of the name, the London Bridge is often confused with the Tower Bridge, which *is* an impressive monument. The most recent incarnation of the London Bridge was inaugurated in 1973. In 1968 an American bought the old bridge when England decided to construct a new London Bridge. Londoners love to say that the American buyer thought that he was buying the Tower Bridge. Britons often like to view America as being the daft little brother of England, who somehow lost the plot. The nineteenth-century London Bridge is now in Lake Havasu City, Arizona—at least some of the stones from it are there. It became the centerpiece for a theme park in the Arizona desert. It is an ersatz structure: a steel-reinforced concrete frame, clad with some of the stones from the original structure.

London is an up-to-date consumer society—business as usual in the pay-as-you-go industrialized world. Following the arbiters of superficial style in the mainstream current is the trend.

Trendy conventionality is the norm. There are many styles and price-of-entry levels available in the marketplace, from the funky sci-fi ambience of Camden Town, to the strained opulence of Harrods Department Store in Knightsbridge. Frankly, there is too much stuff—too many mind-numbing choices. And London *is* expensive.

The architectural environment in London is somewhat disappointing. Things don't look like they did in the old movies. The panoramic view needs to be observed with tunnel vision. The foundations of the culture appear to be as solid as the brick buildings in England, but the ravages of the modern world have taken their toll. The architectural presence of the impressive old buildings is everywhere, but they are interspersed with newer buildings that are less than inspired. The blitzkrieg of World War II destroyed much of the old architecture. Now, classic edifices appear like bits of truffle in a pâté de foie gras. When I emerged from the Tube station, on my first trip into the City of London, I gazed at the Houses of Parliament and Big Ben. Years ago, my first sight of Paris was the Arc de Triomphe. I gazed at it as I emerged from a Metro station, one evening in 1985, with a Frenchwoman on my arm. Paris has done a much better job of preserving the beautiful architectural ambience of that city. Of course, that city did not undergo the blitzkrieg that London did. In England, the French are sometimes referred to as "surrender monkeys." Piccadilly Circus is the Times Square of London. It doesn't hold a candle to Times Square. The largest Ferris wheel in Europe is in London: the London Eye. It is not a rigid-frame wheel; it is a tensile structure—made like a giant bicycle wheel. Decades ago (before he went into his phase of talking to plants), Prince Charles made speeches, imploring architects and city planners to be more sensitive to the architectural ambience of London—to reconsider the trend of constructing intrusive buildings that don't blend in with the traditional old buildings. Apparently, not many people were listening. Today, London is an architectural pastiche.

I am an aberrant New Englander. The pursuit of joie de vivre came naturally to me. Of course, it was inevitable that I would have to leave New England in order to follow this frivolous course in life. Along the way, there have been many wrong turns, blind alleys, and lamentable way stations. Sometimes I hit the bull's-eye. There is a Janus-like, double face to travel: the urge to escape, attached to the impulse to arrive at a desired place. The art of flight is an acquired skill. I began by sneaking away from my New England prep school on Wednesday afternoons during my senior year—at the risk of expulsion. Leaving town was prohibited. In these excursions, I was seeking the company of my girlfriend and a few moments of erotic pleasure. We were in love. She lived in my hometown, which was about thirty miles away from the boarding school that confined me. In these trysts, timing was everything. I didn't want to give up my diploma, after having endured the school up until then. On Wednesdays there was no 5:05 class and no compulsory sports. Immediately after lunch, I would dash to my room and disguise myself, reasonably well—to look like a "townie." I removed my sport coat and tie and put on a waist-length jacket. I turned up the collar of the jacket, to hide my face as much as possible. On these days I was always careful never to wear glen-plaid pants or red socks, but I never went so far as to wear white socks, a clear indicator of "Harry High." Had I been seen sporting this socially tabooed article of clothing, it would certainly have aroused suspicion. One of the two intercity bus stops in the town was in front of a luncheonette that was a short distance from the school. I had cased this restaurant for a while, and I never encountered anyone from the school. It was off the beaten path. "Preppies" didn't go there. After changing my clothes, I would casually walk off campus and make my way to this restaurant. I sat at the formica counter and sipped a Coke while I attentively watched the large, plate-glass window, waiting to see the bus coming around the corner. When I saw the nose of the bus appear, I would bolt out the door and rush toward the sign that indicated the stop, keeping my head down and my collar up. I always sat at the rear of the bus. Once, a teacher from the prep school got on the bus, at the second stop in town. Luckily, he sat in the front of the bus. I had to slouch down in my seat, all the way to Holyoke, where he got off. My girlfriend would meet me at the bus station in Springfield. After taking a city bus to her house, we would go immediately into the basement. There was a daybed there. A couple of orgasms later, it would be time to retrace my way back to the boarding school, put on a jacket and tie, and run to the dining hall, for dinner. These weekly meetings sustained me during that year, but I longed for my commencement.

In the modern world, the experience of life is inextricably linked to consumption. The cost of life is escalating rapidly. Individuals are trapped in the pay-as-you-go life. There are questions being raised, about the sustainability of this trend. And, in the consumer jungle, quite often, there is more sizzle than steak.

7
Out and About
(in search of Englishness)

Having got settled into a routine in my life in "London," I have begun to explore my environs, as much as I can afford. London has a complex and highly efficient public transportation system. Out of the bunker and into the trenches—on the meter. Commerce is deeply intertwined with daily life. My first two excursions into central London had been to do some general sightseeing—getting the lay of the land. The gridded streets of New York are far less confusing than the winding streets of London. It costs money to go around London, and the outlay begins as soon as you go out your door. Not the least of which goes into the tills of pubs. Pubs are a necessary part of life in England, although it seems clear that they have declined in social function. They are probably not what they used to be. Some pubs in London have turned into wine bars.

They have talking buses in London. I am developing a slight infatuation with the woman whose voice announces the bus stops. The way she says "*Tooting* Broadway." One night, a male voice with a cockney accent interrupted the usual progression of announcements, with an update indicating a closed bus stop. It was my stop. I neglected to hear this message and found myself going down a motorway, past my room.

There are understated post-Orwellian overtones in London. Closed-circuit television cameras watch your every move. There are CCTV cameras, literally, everywhere. Police helicopters fly over the city. There is always one close at hand. Occasionally, matte-black, twin-rotor Chinook helicopters fly overhead, at low level. When spring arrived, there was a rumor going around. People were saying that Maypoles had been banned in England—possibly for matters of prurience, but certainly for concerns about "health and safety," as the English call it. It turns out that it is not true. It is a folk myth. But, the complaints about health-and-safety regulations are valid. The British government is obsessed with going overboard, to protect everybody from everything.

One evening, when I was returning home from Kingston, a group of police officers swarmed toward a bus that was arriving at the bus station. They carried small electronic devices that were used to inspect Oyster cards. They were checking to see if the passengers had paid—and the cards contained data about where the passengers had been. Shades of *Nineteen Eighty-Four*.

One afternoon, I observed a heavyset man plodding across a bridge. He was situated in between two Nordic walking poles that he was dragging along with him. Was he training, off-season, for cross-country skiing, or was he ruining his Sunday afternoon stroll? I also saw a man-sized chicken walking down the street in Kingston-upon-Thames, but that was something else. It was a promotion for a fried-chicken takeaway restaurant. This brings up the subject of urban trekking gear: hiking shoes, cargo pants, backpacks, and headphones—and of course, assorted wheeled-objects, such as skateboards and scooters. I saw an adult couple walking their scooters along the sidewalk (or "pavement," as the English call it), in the radical-trendy atmosphere of Camden Town—fully equipped for trekking in the urban jungle that is London.

Rental bicycles have recently been introduced into London. A Copenhagen or an Amsterdam, London is not. The adoption of this progressive urban feature was, perhaps, not prudent in London. Gawking tourists wearing headphones will be a veritable shooting gallery for drivers. Business people deciding to pedal home after unwinding at the pub will be another unwanted presence. The bikes are much cheaper than a taxi. The public backlash has begun. Originally, only available to bankers and other privileged people, the bikes are now accessible to the general public. Arnold Schwarzenegger recently did a photo op while riding one of these bicycles. As private automobiles, taxis, buses, trucks, and professional bicycle couriers vie for their position in the street, this erratic component of traffic may very well cause havoc during the summer tourist season.

I am searching for vestiges of the old London. I see a glutted marketplace, with too many choices. Pity the people on the lower end of the socioeconomic spectrum, struggling to be gratified in the life of consumption. I hear *beeps*—coming from every direction—from other people's mobile phones, my mobile phone, automobile door locks, trucks going in reverse, and pedestrian crossing-lights. Pity the blind people. The first time that I received a text message on my mobile phone here, I thought that the smoke detector in my room had gone off. In London, one can quite frequently hear the Queen's English, spoken with a Valley-girl accent. It is an unnerving presence.

London is a cosmopolitan city, a multicultural city, and a global city. The word *multiculturalism* labels a slippery issue, with hazy boundaries. It is somehow linked to the murky subject of globalism. It is, nevertheless, a buzzword: a slogan for political correctness. The British are grappling with this matter. Britain is a political and economic entity that is composed of three nations that have been fused into one state. The citizens Britain: are they English, Welsh, and Scottish—or British? That is a question the inhabitants of this island ask themselves. In Scotland, the Scots make a distinction between Scottish Highlanders and Scottish Lowlanders. Northern Ireland is not part of Great Britain, but it is part of the United Kingdom. It is on a different island. That relationship is even more controversial. The influx of foreigners is very evident in Britain. London is composed of a hodgepodge of ethnic groups, many of whom come from the Indian subcontinent, the Caribbean, Eastern Europe, and Asia. On London buses, English is often one of the least heard languages.

What is the goal: amalgamation through acculturation or the maintenance of a harmonious cultural mosaic—preserving cultural integrity or evolving into a new multicultural form. In the United States the tendency is toward amalgam. America is a melting pot, but social polarization and internecine squabbling are on the rise. The generic American lifestyle is the prototype for the global consumer society. Cities are conforming to the up-to-date global styles that are beginning to pervade urbanscapes. Globally branded-and-blanded shops serve up the same fare everywhere. Cultures are being diluted. Is English culture fading away? Englishness is certainly taking on a new face. Things change, but the excessively rapid disappearance of cultural forms taking place in the modern world is a recent phenomenon. A recent statistic revealed that thirty-five percent of affluent Brits want to leave Britain because of the lack of sun (sun-seeking impulses), high taxes, and increasing antisocial behavior. What is happening to the real England? I have seen better pseudo-Tudor buildings in America, than I have seen in my neighborhood here in London.

Apropos of nothing, the English love to eat stomach-wrenching Indian cuisine: that chaotic taste sensation caused by a superfluity of spices that are intended to obfuscate the taste of spurious bits of food. Indian restaurants are a ubiquitous presence in England. Apparently, this food appeals to tongue-numbed drunks as well as more sober Brits. One afternoon, I saw an entry on a menu in a pub, which listed a selection of "luxury curries." What is a *luxury* curry? Is it made with swan meat? McGourmet, I say. It's Indian food. The food is the cuisine of an impoverished and refrigeration-deficient culture. Cover-up-the-taste-of-the-meat is a guiding principle. The omnipresence of chili peppers in Mexican cuisine is not without reason.

8
Public Life
(looking for Tom, Dick, and Harry)

Oddly, the English pronounce "Harry," something like the French (whom the English generally make a point of detesting, with an atavistic animosity). They barely pronouncing the *H*. Pubs are a staple of British culture. They are quite different from bars. A pub is a public station, not merely a watering hole. There is a popularly held belief in England, that people in London are disinclined to talk to strangers. There is some truth to this. This characteristic is probably typical of most large cities. The problem is that this kind of behavior turns pubs into mere bars. When speaking to someone in public is regarded as strange behavior, community is waning. The line of demarcation between social acceptability and social unacceptability is a social indicator.

The English café bears little resemblance to a European café. The two have almost nothing in common, except that they are both being supplanted by café-like establishments that are owned by transnational corporations. European cafés are public stations—places to have a drink and socialize. English cafés are like jerry-rigged luncheonettes, without the lunch counter. They serve English breakfasts and things that resemble sandwiches. They are being encroached on by generic commercial chains. Ironically, the Eurocoffee phenomenon, which started in America, has come to Europe. The imitation is being implanted at the source. It is called "Americanization." In the 1980s, Parisian cafés were infamous for their rude anti-American waiters. At least they were cafés.

My "local" pub is two bus rides away, in Richmond-upon-Thames. It is the only pub that I have found where people talk to each other. A sad state of affairs for London. The bus fare to get to my pub and back is the equivalent of two pints of beer. There is a rich *use* of the English language in Britain. Wit is a skill that is learned at an early age. Never have I lived so far from my café—except on occasions when I lived in America, and the café was on the other side of the Atlantic Ocean.

On weekends, there are black-clad security guards in the McDonald's in Kingston-upon-Thames—to make sure that some kid doesn't throw a pickle at someone. One Saturday night, as I was returning home from Kingston, with a double cheeseburger in my hand, there were seven or eight youths at the bus stop. It was at one of the two bus stations in that town. They were evidently interested in me. There was no one else at the bus stop, and it was nearly midnight. One of the group stood up and acted as though he was the leader of the pack. He sneered at me. Being an American, I have relatively good street sense. They weren't just a few lads having a good laugh. What they were was something else. At the second bus station in Kingston, I got off the bus—at the last minute. My home bus stop is in a desolate industrial area. They were on the upper deck of the double-decker bus. I sat on the lower level, near to the door. As the bus took off, they noticed me standing on the sidewalk. I smiled.

    Civil unrest has started in London. Riots have broken out. Today is the fourth day of the sickening violence. It is August 9, 2011. Last night, there were riots five miles down the road from where I live. The riots started in north London. They have been moving in a pincer pattern around Outer London. The Internet is being used to organize the attacks. False attacks are organized in order to attract the police, before the main attack takes place elsewhere. I am just beyond the front line of the internecine terrorism, in southwest London. The police came into the neighborhood this afternoon and told the owners of restaurants and shops, to close their doors by seven o'clock, at the latest. Police intelligence indicated that gangs may be moving into this neighborhood between seven and eight o'clock. The is no police presence in the street. It is now seven-thirty. This is London, but it suddenly seems like a city in North Africa or the Middle East.

The police do not seem to know what they're doing. The British government directed the police to stand down while murder, mayhem, arson, and looting took place. While the rioting was taking place, the people legitimately empowered to protect the population did *nothing*. It is obscenely disgraceful. The police didn't even attempt to defend the people that they are paid to protect. The government says that it doesn't want to call out the military. If this were America, the National Guard would be in the streets by now. The British politicians are conversing at this very moment. I am waiting to see what happens next. The rioting is about looting and vandalism. It is consumer anarchy—the result of social degeneration. The hooligan sociopaths think that they don't have enough stuff. One teenage girl said, as she was taking swigs from a bottle of wine that she had looted, "We're showing the rich that we can do what we want."

The night passed quietly. Occasionally, squadrons of police vans raced by, with sirens blaring. Anyway, there isn't much worth looting in my neighborhood. There were riots in other English cities. Today, there were record sales of baseball bats in England.

England is the land of bunny huggers and fox hunters. Fox hunting has been banned. Bunny hugging is still in full swing.

9
Only the Queen Can Eat Swans

Being from "across the pond," I was shocked to find out that, until quite recently, a person could be imprisoned in the Tower of London, for killing one of the Queen's swans. All of the swans in Britain belong to her. Having seen the Tower of London, I surmise that this course of action would not be the worst recourse, for a life in London. The Tower of London is one of the more beautiful buildings in London—high-end real estate, right on the Thames River. The cost of housing in London is exorbitant. Many people live in rooms that they rent. The cost of these rooms, with shared facilities, is enough to pay for a comfortable apartment in most places in America. Housing in London is being restructured toward a goal of producing warrens of cramped, rentable living spaces. There are a lot of renovations taking place. In London, beds can be purchased with three-year loans. Some Europeans refer to London as being the New York of Europe. In my estimation, it is more like the Boston of Europe. Many people who are employed in Boston commute inordinately long distances because they cannot afford to live anywhere near to the city in which they work. London is expensive, and the quality of things being offered in the marketplace is frequently disappointing—particularly the obligatorily-prepaid, overcooked, stone cold, ten-dollar hamburgers that are plunked down on your table, by rude and indifferent waiters in pubs.

Standards of living vary in London. There is a purchasing-power struggle taking place in the marketplace. The fashionable West End of London is a place known for flaunting conspicuous consumption. In that section of London there is an efflorescence of luxury consumables. In other places in London, there are staggering numbers of superficial variations of less expensive consumables. I was with a friend when she bought a Duncan Imperial yo-yo from Harrods, the famous luxury department store, in the West End of London. The store has faux Egyptian undertones, in its interior decor. There were yo-yos in ancient Greece. There is a yo-yo shown on a fifth-century BC Grecian urn. In 1962, when I was in the sixth grade, Duncan yo-yos were a fad in America. Every kid had one. And they worked. In 2011 the overpriced yo-yo bought from Harrods didn't work. It went down, but it didn't come up again. The loop of the string that was attached to the axle of the yo-yo was too loose. Apparently, there is a problem with quality control, these days. The yo-yo looked the same as it had in 1962, but it wasn't the same.

There are white vans everywhere on the roadways in England. They are the vehicle of choice, for workers who move from job to job. Why are they almost always white? Perhaps it is because they are more anonymous—less easy to be identified. ("Oh! He was driving a white van. That's all I can remember.") In England, there are invisible cameras, which record speeding violations. The driving-style of white-van drivers is the subject of controversy (or con-trah-versy, as they say in England). The white vans are all racing to their next job. Time is money in the rat race. There is no time to lose.

In ancient Athens, the original democracy came about because the masses of people had been reduced to virtual slavery, while the elites had sumptuous and opulent lifestyles. The seeds of revolution had sprouted, and the elites were a little nervous about the social atmosphere.

    The Ford Model T was the first car produced for the masses. Before the Model T, only the rich owned automobiles. There was concern among the elites, that envy for automobiles might cause social unrest in the United States.

One afternoon, as I sipped a pint of ale in a pub, I watched part of a session of the House of Commons, which was being broadcast on television. It was far less impressive than the sight of the Houses of Parliament. Two Members of Parliament were debating trash-removal systems. One would think that that ought to be a municipal issue. The two elected officials were bickering with each other. The issue revolved around the merits of the various ways of recycling chicken tikka leftovers. The point in question was whether this garbage should be used to feed hungry people, or be converted into biofuel. One Member of Parliament asked another MP, what she thought should be done with leftover chicken tikka (a popular Indian takeaway menu item). In reply, the other politician indignantly denied that she ate chicken tikka. But, she acknowledged that she was aware of this dish; her children ate it. In order to avoid taking a position on the topic, her argument was that there were never any chicken tikka leftovers in her house. *Her* children *always* cleaned their plates. Perhaps, the politicians in Britain should be more concerned with the radioactive waste that has been piling up in Sellafield, in Cumbria, for decades. The nuclear facility at Sellafield is one of the world's biggest nuclear dump sites. Another instance of the effect of Indian food on British culture.

I recently had to get a new prescription for some medication. As a foreigner in England, I am prohibited from going to a doctor who is associated with the National Health Service in this country. I searched the Internet and found that there was only one private doctor in the part of London where I live. His office was two bus rides away. I called the office and made an appointment. When I arrived at the doctor's office, I noticed that there was an Aston Martin parked in his driveway. I was charged eighty pounds (one hundred thirty dollars) for a five-minute consultation. I offered to pay him in cash, on the spot, but he insisted that it was "more civilized" for him to send me a bill in the mail. I received the bill, a few days after my visit to the doctor. The bill indicated that it was to be paid within fourteen days, otherwise interest would be added. When I called the doctor's office, to arrange payment, using a credit card, I was told that there was a four percent surcharge, for payments made with credit cards. On the other hand, the prescription cost me one twentieth as much as it would have cost in the United States.

In London everybody seems to be trying to grab money from someone else. It is becoming a dog-eat-dog city. Urban life is becoming increasingly unviable, for the servile class.

Cities, as settlement forms in the globalizing world, are losing their individual characters. Urban centers are being transformed into generic variations of Any City. England appears to be like the smartest of *The Three Little Pigs*. In London there is still some brickwork left in evidence. Brick buildings don't deteriorate as easily as wood-framed buildings, such as there are in America. Having said that, there are wood-framed buildings in England that go back to Shakespeare's time. Some of the past architecture remains. Hopefully, some of the cultural brickwork still remains in the collective unconscious of England. In London the brick buildings of the past stand beside the glass-and-steel structures of the present. The cost of labor is a factor in this architectural transformation. Many of the post-World War II buildings in London deserve to be torn down. What could the architects have been thinking? Not much, evidently.

There is a building that is conspicuous on the London skyline. It is called "The Gherkin." This skyscraper is a London landmark. The building doesn't look anything like a pickle. It is a politically correct nickname for a building that resembles a giant bullet pointing upward toward heaven. There is a problem with renting the offices in the building. The upper floors are not particularly well thought-out spaces for inhabitation by human beings. The architectural monument craze is flourishing in some places in the world. Inordinately expensive wristwatches and skyscrapers are status symbols in the global economy. At the present time, the Chinese and various petroleum-producing countries in the Middle East are the major sponsors for the architectural designs of ever-taller skyscrapers, which are meant to impress us all. I can imagine God saying to the Lord Mayor of

London, "Is that a pickle in your city center, or are you glad to see me?"

Overview

10
Leaf Peeping

While driving through the foliage in the Berkshires of western Massachusetts, on a trip to the United States in October 2008, I smelled an odor coming through the ventilation system of my rental car. I peered suspiciously at the automobile that was up ahead of me. Smoke was pouring out of the tailpipe of the car. The fumes smelled like the discharge that comes out of exhaust fans in fast-food restaurants. A sign was prominently displayed on the back of the vehicle: THIS CAR RUNS ON RECYCLED VEGETABLE OIL. Just as I was reading this, I thought I caught a glimpse of a turnip truck, on the road up ahead. The car running on used french-fry oil was poking along at well below the speed limit, and the smell that it was emitting was becoming increasingly annoying. It was interfering with my long-awaited leaf peeping. This caused me to punch down on the gas pedal of the Mustang and engage the turbocharger, thus spewing a blast of hydrocarbons into the atmosphere as I passed the eco-vehicle. I thought: what if the other side of the sociological coin in America were to start running their cars on biofuel made from recycled, egested granola? Where would that get us? The United States government would be impelled to pass regulations requiring Beano (an anti-flatulence product) to be an additive in granola. This could cause a Beano shortage. Natural-food restaurants would have to install electricity-consuming flatulence extractors, which would possibly lead to the production of more nuclear power plants, in order to meet increasing energy demands. Ordinances could erupt in some places, requiring diners who are eating in public establishments, to consume their legumes and sulfurous vegetables on the sidewalk in front of the restaurant. Supermarkets might be forced to display warning labels on cabbages: *for the consideration of those around you, please consume this vegetable in a well-ventilated place.*

Continuing northward into Vermont, in pursuit of colorful leaves, I cruised down a route in the middle of nowhere. The desolate country road was lined with faded and frayed American flags, flying from the tops of telephone poles. The foliage was a little beyond its peak. Things seemed to be a bit bleak. I said to my friend, who was traveling with me: "See one leaf, and you've seen them all. Let's get out of here." I consulted a map and turned onto the most direct route leading to Interstate 91, to return to Massachusetts.

A few days later, I was in New York City. After an elevator trip up to the top of the Empire State Building, I stood looking out over and down at Manhattan. This skyscraper was the tallest building in New York until the World Trade Center was built. The Chrysler Building had been the tallest building in Manhattan (for eleven months) until the construction of the Empire State Building was completed in 1931. Standing on the observation deck of the Empire State Building, looking toward Lower Manhattan, I thought I saw golden parachutes flying out of the windows of some buildings in the vicinity of Wall Street. The stock market had just taken a big plunge downward. At that time the Icelandic economy was twittering away, like a canary in a coal mine. Times change. During a heavy fog in 1945, a B-25 bomber crashed into the Empire State Building—between the 79th and 80th floors. One of the engines shot through the building and landed on the roof of a building on the next block, incinerating a penthouse: a sculptor's studio. Two days later, some floors in the Empire State Building were in use.

My friend, who is from Yorkshire, England, used the occasion of standing in the long line waiting for the first of the two elevators used to go down to the ground floor of the Empire State Building, to give a rather audible and overly protracted speech concerning the nature of obsessive-compulsive disorder. He concluded that, at its root, this is essentially a condition of "being afraid to live." There was subsequently some nervous rustling in the crowd.

The Grand Central Oyster Bar & Restaurant, located in Grand Central Station, is a landmark. It is a New York institution and a great place to kill some time while waiting for a train. The day that my friend and I were waiting for a train to go to New Haven, there were thirty-five different oysters on the menu. After sliding down some Blue Points and Wellfleets, we moved on to devour Moonstones and Hama-Hamas.

After the snack at the Oyster Bar, there was time for one more beer, at the bar on the mezzanine that overlooks the main hall of Grand Central Station. When we had seated ourselves on stools at the bar, my friend asked the bartender, "What's that thing doing hanging from the ceiling?" That "thing" was a huge American flag that was obstructing the view of the beautiful vaulted ceiling of the recently restored edifice, corrupting the architectural space—or at least that's what my friend said to the shocked bartender, who, when he heard the question, nervously glanced around at the other customers at the bar, with a look on his face that indicated he had no idea how to reply.

One of the great joys of New England is the seafood there. I grew up with it. Newport, Rhode Island, seemed like an opportune place to eat a couple of lobsters. Twenty-seven years earlier, I had lived in Little Compton, Rhode Island. At that time Newport was a touristic place during the summer months, but it had many cozy bars and traditional seafood restaurants. Now, Newport is full of posh shops and luxurious restaurants, catering to those inclined to consume conspicuously. In 2008, restaurants were serving lobsters, garnished with strange béchamel sauces. Men in suits and ties and women in chic dresses stood outside of these restaurants, posing with their credit cards. I have nothing against béchamel sauce, but it seems inappropriate—for lobsters that have just been hauled out of the sea—serving only to mask the delicate flavor of this delicious crustacean. And, linen tablecloths are impractical and ostentatious pretensions for an inherently messy meal. After wandering around for a few minutes, we found what was one of the last of the old seafood restaurants in Newport. A blackboard mounted on the wall just outside the entrance indicated that a twin-lobster special was being offered. The restaurant had interesting beers on tap. When taking our order, the owner lamented the changes that had taken place in his town. When four boiled lobsters had been placed in front of us, my friend asked me, "How do you eat these?" He had never eaten a lobster before.

"Like this," I replied, as I tore off a large claw and cracked it open, with a nutcracker. It had been a few years since I had eaten one of these culinary delights. They were soft-shell lobsters, preferable for both texture and flavor. October is a peak time in the year for lobsters. The water is cold.

In the middle of the meal, I turned away from my lobsters and said something out loud to the television, which was hung above the bar. The television was airing a presidential debate. My comment had something to do with the vapidness of what was being said by the candidates. My friend glanced around the bar. The only others in there, except for the bartender and the owner, were a few customers who were drinking at the end of the bar. My friend from Yorkshire proceeded to tell me that I couldn't say what I had said. As I was cracking open another lobster claw, I replied, "In the United States, we have a constitutional right to free speech." After the meal, we went to a fisherman's bar down the street and had a drink with the other customers, who were not in the least offended by my comments.

11
Obsolescence
(a lament for the clipper ship)

In the nineteenth century, clipper ships were state-of-the-art sailing vessels. They sailed all over the world, carrying high-profit freight, such as spices, tea, silk, people, and mail. With their narrow, sleek hulls, and concave, raked bows that cut through waves, they were the fastest cargo ships of their time. Clipper ships had large sail areas, relative to the size of their hulls. They carried less freight than other sailing vessels. The China clippers were the fastest commercial sailing vessels ever made. In the aftermath of the Panic of 1857, an economic crisis of the nineteenth century, the use of the clipper ship began to decline. In the latter half of the nineteenth century, some hybrid steam clippers were built, but the gradual introduction of the steamship would eventually render the clipper ship obsolete.

It was a period of prosperity. The postwar economic boom that followed the accelerated wartime economy resulted in economic growth, which was fed from increasing consumer spending. Assembly-line mass production was providing a marvelous array of new consumer goods. Things that had previously been the privilege of the wealthy were being made available to the middle class. Planned obsolescence was developed as a way of ensuring the ongoing consumption of products. Radio was the first mass broadcasting medium. It provided a vehicle for mass marketing. The masses were being acculturated to a new phase of consumerism and the way of life associated with it. There was widespread enthusiasm about modern technology and the wonders that it was making possible. Paying for household goods over time, allowed the purchasing of big-ticket items, which would have been unaffordable to many. Debt was assumed in order to purchase stocks in the booming stock market. "Buying on margin" became a buzzword on Wall Street. Availability of credit and investor overconfidence led to a speculative bubble on Wall Street. Then the stock market crashed. It was the Roaring Twenties.

It has been said that the two things that distinguish humans from other animals are opposable thumbs and the ability to produce articulated, complex language. Humans were provided with the ability to make tools and to talk to each other. Early on, humans discovered the way to make fire.

In neolithic cultures, tools were made primarily from stone. Fired ceramics, agriculture, and animal husbandry were innovations of neolithic culture. The ability to cultivate food and store it efficiently provided the means for humans to live in permanent houses in settlements, replacing a way of life that entailed moving from place to place, living in temporary huts, and searching for wild food sources.

At the dawn of Civilization humans were making the elementary mechanical object, known as the wheel.

In the late eighteenth century and the nineteenth century, during the Industrial Revolution, machine tools and the factory system gradually replaced hand tools and artisanship. Mass-produced consumer goods, manufactured in factories, replaced handcrafted products made in cottage industries. Fossil-fuel-powered steam engines would replace wind, water, horse, and human power. Canals and railways were made, to facilitate commerce. Electric power generation and the internal combustion engine would be developed. Mass production was a quantum leap in consumerism.

In the 1950s there was a ratcheting up of consumerism. Planned obsolescence, in function and style, was a key manufacturing strategy. At that time, my mother purchased our groceries at the Plumtree Food Shop. It was a few blocks away from our house, in suburbia. The grocery store was housed in a quaint-looking brick building. In those days milk trucks still delivered milk, fresh from the dairy, to milk boxes, which were outside kitchen doors. The Plumtree was a cozy store, with one checkout lane at the front. At the back of the store, there was a butcher, who sold *prime* meats. At that time there were supermarkets in existence. They had been around America since the 1930s, but in the 1950s, they began to proliferate. The supermarket that was just beyond the end of our street was called the First National. In those days supermarkets were much smaller than today's supermarkets—but they were a lot bigger than the Plumtree. Supermarkets had a cold, impersonal atmosphere, and they sold *choice* meats: a lower grade of meat. Among the items on the shelves along the aisles of the Plumtree, there were exotic canned goods from England. Eventually, the Plumtree would go out of business. It couldn't compete with the supermarkets. When larger supermarkets came into existence, smaller supermarkets would be phased out. When it comes to marketplace forms, America has a tendency to throw out the baby with the bath water.

Five-and-dime stores were common features of main streets in cities and towns in 1950s America. The inside of these stores had a peculiar smell. The bolts of fabrics and the lunch counter contributed to the distinct aroma. Some of these five-and-dimes had pneumatic tube systems. There was an office, with a cashier, perched like an eagle's nest, overlooking the store. When a customer's payment was given to a clerk in the store, it was put into a cylindrical capsule, which was then shot up to the office, via a clear tube. The customer's change would be returned, the same way.

In the late 1950s, discount department stores came onto the American scene. These were usually built on commercially-zoned strips of roadway, on the outskirts of cities and towns. These proto-big-box stores would eventually displace the dime stores, only to be eventually pushed aside, as larger stores came along.

After the demise of the Plumtree Food Shop, in the late 1960s, my mother moved out of my hometown in Massachusetts and went to live in a small town in Maine. This town still had a butcher—who sold prime meats. It also had a supermarket, as well as many small shops, located along the main street. When this butcher retired, there was no butcher in town or in the area. My mother was forced to buy prepackaged "choice" meat at the supermarket.

In the 1990s, the most famous of all big box stores built one of their establishments on the outskirts of the town where my mother lived. The well-known big box store had been down the road for some time before my mother decided to venture to go into it. By this time, many of the small shops in the town had closed their doors. When she came home from this short excursion, my mother had a disgusted look on her face. She had one comment about her shopping expedition: "The inside of the store smelled like body odor and stale popcorn. I'll never go in there again." As far as I know, she never did. She was still peeved about the disappearance of the local butcher.

12
Furniture
(a personal view)

My reductionist definition of furniture is: something that has a horizontal surface. From my standpoint, I reduce all reasonably-sized, movable objects, to seats and tables—and beds, which are somewhat ambiguous surfaces during waking hours. And then there are *ornaments*, those all too conveniently transportable objects. They are one of the banes of my life. There is an expression (quite possibly concocted by a disorderly person) that states that an orderly house is the sign of a disorganized mind, and vice versa. I doubt that it is quite that clear-cut.

I have a propensity for creating clutter on tables. Tidiness is not my forte. The fewer tables, the better. Any horizontal surface is just asking to be a receptacle for the material residua of my day-to-day life. Who said that the computer was going to lead to a paperless life?

Knowing my proclivity, I am inclined toward minimalism, with regard to furniture. Ornaments are, for me, grotesque and superfluous presences: intentionally created clutter. I have never aspired to a life of dusting knick-knacks. I don't particularly like clutter, thus hotels are an ideal living environment for me. In hotels the clutter magically disappears from the room, every afternoon. The chambermaids mysteriously separate the trash from the important bits, and toss it away. And the furniture in a hotel room has nothing to do with me. It's just there, to be used—and it will be there when I have left the hotel.

In my lifetime I have seen the American "living room" devolve, transmuting from a sitting room, into a quasi-bedroom-cum-dining room—an upholstered lounge. The introduction of the television apparently had something to do with this phenomenon. Sofas and recliner armchairs are siren-like magnets for indolence: breeding grounds for videotropism: directional growth in response to a tendency inclined toward a particular type of behavior. Sadly, in America, the dining table has become a somewhat moribund piece of furniture.

In furnishings, I distinguish between instruments and decorative objects. This distinction runs along a rather nebulous spectrum, between utility and gimcrackery. Suffice it to say that gewgaws, whatnots, and doodads are not my cup of tea. They are tolerable—if they belong to someone else. Memorabilia is another thing. Unfortunately, many of these mementos get lost along the way. (How hotel chambermaids are able to tell the difference between—in the clutter of the daily debris—the memorabilia and the waste paper, I don't know.)

Furniture is generally defined as being large, movable equipment. *Baggage* is portable equipment. To *furnish* is to equip with what is necessary or desirable. The distinction between instrumentality and ornamentation is a bit blurred.

Style is a matter of taste. In my childhood the typical, fashionable choices available in furniture stores were: New England colonial, Danish modern, French provincial, and generic contemporary. The Dutch mode of interior decor is defined by the term *gezellig:* meaning a cozy, relaxing, comfortable, friendly atmosphere. Knick-knacks clutter Dutch interiors.

The minimalism of the nineteenth-century Japanese house has appealed to me, from the very first time that I saw photos of these dwellings. There is no furniture in sight. The floor, in effect, is a piece of furniture: a seat. The floor is covered with tatami mats. When a table or a bed is needed, it is taken out of a closet and then replaced back out of the way when it is not needed. Lightweight, sliding wall-panels facilitate the creation of different, temporary room spaces. I shudder to think about the clutter on the tatami mats, if I were to live in one of these dwellings. The size of *that* horizontal surface.

The *decor*, the furnishing and decoration of a room, is the result of the accidental and intended process of furnishing—the incremental accumulation of furnishings.

When I was a child, my mother had a friend who had a living room in her house that was off limits. It seemed to be cordoned off with invisible velvet ropes. The whole living room existed as an ornament, intended to be used only on the rarest of occasions—or perhaps not at all. I once sat in this room, with my mother and her friend. I don't remember the occasion that prompted this invitation. Perhaps my mother's friend thought that we should sit in there, at least once. The furniture was contemporary in style. It was a very attractive room. I sat beside my mother, on the couch. I had the feeling that I shouldn't be sitting on the furniture. The room was museum-like. There was a beautiful ashtray on the middle of the coffee table. When my mother lit up a cigarette and attempted to put the burnt match into the ashtray, my mother's friend quickly got up from her chair and grabbed the ashtray, taking it out of my mother's reach. "I'll get one from the kitchen," she said, as she dashed out of the room—before the ash on the cigarette became precariously long.

There was a zoo in my hometown. This zoo featured a "monkey house," which contained cages of various lower primates, who were usually screeching or picking at each other (or worse). The building also housed some lions and tigers that were caged alongside the monkeys. When you first walked into this building, it stank like hell inside. After a few minutes, you didn't notice the smell. This phenomenon is explained by the term *habituation:* the diminishing of a response to a frequently repeated stimulus.

The traditional Japanese house has a tokonoma: an alcove, to display ornaments, such as a flower arrangement and a scroll. The things placed in the tokonoma are changed frequently—they are a temporary presence. They are replaced in the closet when the aesthetic affect begins to diminish.

Something that is "part of the furniture" is a thing that has been somewhere so long that it seems to be a permanent, unquestioned, or invisible feature. When does "baggage"—past experiences or long-held ideas that are regarded as being burdens and impediments—become part of the decor? Rentable storage spaces are available, to serve as receptacles for the overflow.

Anyway, that's my mental furniture, regarding furniture.

13
What Happened to Christmas?

Twas the night before Christmas, and not a creature was stirring—except for the bean counters in the financial districts. These creatures were guzzling Champagne while they eagerly awaited for the outcome of the Christmas shopping season. As the media frequently points out, consumer spending accounts for seventy percent of the gross domestic product of the United States. The two months before Christmas are very profitable, for the producers of consumer goods. At the end of the 1950s, the mass media were exuding lamentations about the increasing commercialization of Christmas and the loss of "the true spirit" of the day. No longer. Now, the media talks about numbers. The spirit of Christmas has been lost behind the superficial trappings. Christmas is not what it once was.

In the hazy recesses of my mind, I can remember the excitement that I felt as a child when I went to bed on Christmas Eve—anticipating the morning to come. When I opened my eyes on Christmas morning, I experienced an immeasurable thrill as I jumped out of bed and dashed into the living room, to see what Santa had left under the Christmas tree.

When I was two, Santa Claus brought me a red wagon—a *Radio Flyer*. That year, when it was time for Christmas dinner, I insisted that someone chauffeur me out of the living room. I sat in the wagon, holding onto my yellow security blanket, while my father pulled the wagon into the dining room. I was thinking about how cozy Santa Claus must have been in his sleigh, flying through the sky—with a blanket tucked around him.

The following year, I received a blue pedal car (made from metal, in those days). This gift wasn't from Santa Claus, it was from my aunt Janet. That year, I refused to get out of the car all day. I even insisted on eating my dinner while sitting in the toy car. (Or so my parents told me.) At age three, my legs were not long enough to reach the pedals. A plywood seat-extension had been fashioned, so that I could pedal the car. It was my aunt Jan who, fifteen years later, would buy me my first real car—a 1969 Mustang Mach 1. I ate in numerous drive-ins, in that car.

When I was four years old, we ate Christmas dinner at my grandmother's house. My grandmother was very aesthetically-minded, and she was an exceptionally good cook. Sunday drives with her, always passed through landscapes that were more beautiful than anything that I had ever seen. My grandmother's house was New England colonial-style, inside and out. On this Christmas Day the only light in the dining room came from the electric candles on the window sills and the candles burning on the dining table. The turkey dinner was brought in from the kitchen, through the swinging door, and placed onto the table. In the dimly-lit dining room, the candlelight flickered on the faces of my family, while we ate the delicious food. It was snowing outside.

Toys ought not to be about making the global economy spin around in circles. Santa Claus doesn't make toys for the profit-takers—he makes them for children. Toys are not meant to be something to be measured on an accountant's balance sheet. With the increasing commercialization of human culture, quality has given way to quantity. The desire for accumulation has become more important than the joy of appreciating one wondrous thing. More and more is less.

One-cent gum-ball machines have given way to machines that dispense two-dollar plastic capsules containing colorful, gimcrack baubles. Their enticing outer appearance disguises the disappointing inner contents—all sizzle and no gum. The marketing of unfulfilled promises of gratification—for children.

Violent, video war-games, which reward players for committing atrocities that are considered to be war crimes, in violation of international humanitarian law, are being sold as "toys." Joy to the World!

In 1897 Francis Church, a reporter for the newspaper, the New York Sun, received a letter from an eight-year-old girl, named Virginia. She asked him if Santa Claus really existed. Mr. Church had been a war correspondent during the American Civil War. In his answer, which was published in the newspaper, he said: "Yes, Virginia, there is a Santa Claus." His reply is the most reprinted newspaper editorial in the English language.

Yes, there is a Santa Claus, but what have we done to him. Sad to say, in recent decades we have not been very kind to him. And what about the children? Santa Claus doesn't make toys with a profit-motive in his mind. Santa Claus exists only as much as he is in our hearts—in order "to make glad the heart of childhood."

14
Reading

How many a man has dated a new era in his life from the reading of a book.
Henry David Thoreau

In ancient Greece, literacy became commonplace for the first time. It was the beginning of the book. Reading became a pastime. Philosophers and thinkers began to write books. In those days books were usually in the form of scrolls. In history, it is called "the Greek Miracle." In earlier civilizations, only scribes, who were a professional class, were literate. In the first century AD the codex book was developed by the Romans. This book form would gradually replace the scroll. About 1440, Gutenberg's mechanical printing press made codex books available to the masses. Before Gutenberg's printing press, a single book in the Cambridge University library had the economic value of a farm. The codex is now beginning to be replaced with e-books.

At age eight I began avidly reading books, after having learned to read in school, with Dick and Jane and Spot, the dog. The first book that I actually *read* was *Old Mother West Wind,* by Thornton Burgess. My maternal grandmother gave me that book. She had read it when she was a child. Thornton Burgess lived in a country house, located just outside of my hometown. Sometimes, on Sunday drives, I would be taken by his house. There was a grass-covered hillock on his property, which had a window on one side. Inside the turf-covered mound, there was a small room where he wrote his books. His stories are about animals. He observed the animals on his property, from the inside of his cozy bunker. For more than a year, Thornton Burgess books were my bedtime reading.

When I was a child, I also read comic books. Every week I would get two or three comic books. I would read them and then put them on top of the pile of comic books that I had on the floor of my bedroom closet. When the pile got large enough (about eighteen inches would do), I would eagerly wait for a rainy day. When that day came, I would read the pile of comics, in succession, while sitting on my bed. On those days I ate my lunch on the bed. I didn't want to interrupt the reading process. It was a comic book marathon. The thing was this: after a couple of hours of reading the comic books, the visual imagery became more intense. It was as though I was in comicbookland.

The first book that changed my life as an adult was *Walden*, by Henry David Thoreau. I first read this book at age fifteen, but I only understood it, based on what the master at my prep school had explained about it. At age nineteen, when I was studying architecture, I began reading it again, a page every day, while I sat in a grassy field on the campus. On May 4, 1970, four university students were shot and killed at Kent State University, in Ohio, by members of the Ohio National Guard—during a demonstration against the Vietnam War. Immediately after this event, there was a student strike at many American universities. Four million students participated in the strike. At my school, it was necessary to submit a written declaration to the administration of the school, stating that the reason for refusing to attend classes was to work for peace. In my statement, I indicated that I intended to work for "inner peace." With my extra time, I finished reading *Walden*. Five months later, I was conscripted to go into the military. I was not allowed to enter the army because they found me to be "psychologically unfit" for military service.

My aunt Adeline was an avid reader. The large, round table next to her chair in the living room of her house was piled high with books, and there was always a fresh pot of hot coffee in the kitchen. She would sit in her chair for hours, drinking coffee, smoking cigarettes, and reading. The picture window behind her had a view of Provin Mountain. There was a television station perched on the top of the mountain. The antenna for the station flashed its red light, day and night. Aunt Adeline loved to talk about what she was reading. She had an infectious enthusiasm and a laugh that someone who didn't know her might have taken to be slightly sarcastic. It wasn't sarcasm. They were lighthearted laughs, with a witty edge. I always enjoyed visiting my aunt Adeline.

In 1985 I made my first trip to Paris. I went there with a Frenchwoman. I was living with her in Le Cannet, which is just above Cannes, in the south of France. When she had to return home, for her work, I spent a few days alone in Paris. Every day, I wandered the streets of the city. It is easy to get lost in Paris. The streets are labyrinthine—not like the city of New York, where the streets are laid out in a grid, and it is impossible to get lost. One day, on one of my walks in Paris, I suddenly found myself on the Boulevard Haussmann. Marcel Proust lived on this street when he wrote his great literary work, from the seclusion of his bed. I looked up at the building that was in front of me, and there it was: *102,* the number of his house. Shortly thereafter, I read *À la Recherche du Temps Perdu*—in English.

In the course of my life, there have been several books that have changed my life, but none more enduringly than *Walden*.

15
Copenhagen
(proof of the pudding)

I made a trip to Copenhagen in September of 2009. I hadn't been to that city since 1997. Copenhagen is my favorite city in Europe.

Copenhagen is a clean, bright, peaceful city. It is not heavy with the past, nor dingy with the present. There is a lightness to the culture. The architecture is beautiful. The environment is not overburdened with signs or other commercial manifestations, intruding on the ambience. The food is delicious and healthy. Sandwiches are an art form. There are quaint, cobblestone streets lining the city, and there are ornate copper spires rising above the city, pointing upward toward the sky. Pedestrian walkways have textured paving blocks and brass strips: brail pavement. There are parks, lakes, and canals in the city center. There are thousands of bicycles: city bikes, three-wheeled pram trikes for transporting babies and toddlers, rickshaw taxi-trikes, cargo bikes, and assorted other hybrid bicycle forms. There are bicycle lanes throughout the city, with their own traffic lights. Sausage vendors are ubiquitous in the city, selling varieties of tasty *pølse* from their mobile booths. You squirt your favorite garnish onto a piece of wax paper and eat the sausage with your fingers. The vendors move the motorized booths into place, holding onto a long handle, with a throttle attached. A bronze statue of Hans Christian Andersen's "Little Mermaid" graces the entrance to a canal that leads into the city. The internal courtyard of the Queen's palace is a pedestrian walkway. The Danes are friendly and polite. Manners and social function are high priorities in the culture. Danes are inclined give outsiders polite reminders, concerning social conduct. Inherent to the cultural ideology is the idea that nobody should think that they are better than anyone else. There is a national sense of community: a society based on cooperation, not competition. The country is like a national village. In Copenhagen there is a palpable feeling of movement, a chilled-out dynamism. Denmark is said to be the happiest nation on Earth. Denmark has an extraordinary quality of life.

Danish design is renowned. This creative impulse is evident in the sociopolitical system, the urban planning and infrastructure, the architecture, and everyday objects. The Danes have a well thought-out material culture and way of life. In their progress, they consider the nature of the cultural mechanism.

The Danish have a certain reserve when conversing with foreigners. If they know that you know something about their culture, they will open up to you. If you take an ethnocentric and ignorant position regarding their way of life, they will politely ignore you. Danes are modest about their good fortune to be living in Denmark. There is no chest-pounding jingoism. Danes joke about the tallest mountain in Denmark: it rises to 173 meters above sea level. And Danish women are stunningly beautiful.

Denmark has the oldest monarchy in Europe. Denmark has been rated as the least corrupt country in the world. It became a constitutional monarchy in 1894. At that time Danish thinkers designed an egalitarian sociopolitical system. Today, it is the most egalitarian industrialized country in the world. The differential in income level is much smaller than it is in other industrialized countries. Denmark has a parliamentary system of government. The democratic system has multiple parties. The role of political leaders is to be functionaries who oil the machinery—as opposed to being innovators who feel the need to revamp things. (If it ain't broke—don't fix it.) University education is free. Poverty is nonexistent. There are about five and a half million people in Denmark. The name Copenhagen means "merchant's harbor." Maersk, the largest container shipping company in the world, has its headquarters in Copenhagen.

Although Denmark is part of the European Union, they did not join the eurozone. The Danes retained their own currency, the krone. The Danes do pay a lot of taxes, but they do not complain about this imposition, because of the benefits that are returned to them. The Danes know that they can't fall between the cracks and become homeless. There is a two hundred percent tax on the purchase of automobiles. Cars are not a vital necessity in Denmark. The country has an excellent public transportation system. Oddly, the United Nations, in its 2009 Human Development Report, which measures the quality of life, did not include Denmark in its top ten countries.

The two oldest amusement parks in the world are in Copenhagen. Tivoli Gardens is located in the city center. It is an amusement park and a pleasure garden. I swung on a swing, twirling around in a circle, ten stories above the city. I rode on a state-of-the-art roller coaster, clutching at my wallet, to keep it from falling out when I was upside down. My only complaint was that the ride was over too soon. I watched a sound-and-light show, with lasers synchronized to classical music, flashing over a pond in Tivoli. The evening that I went, it was the last day of the season for Tivoli. The evening culminated with a spectacular fireworks display—in the middle of the city of Copenhagen.

Things have changed in Denmark. Night life was, in the old days, the best that I had ever experienced. In the past, at the end of Friday nights and Saturday nights, the Town Hall Square was packed with thousands of revelers, eating sausages and socializing. Now, Danes are staying at home, cocooning with their families, like Americans do. A pint of beer now costs about ten American dollars in Copenhagen. On this last trip, I passed through the Town Hall Square, early Sunday morning, at the end of a Saturday night. I was in a rickshaw that was being peddled by a Russian. The square was empty and dark. A few pedestrians were wandering through. I asked the driver about the scene. He didn't remember ever having seen crowds of people there, at that time of night.

The presence of crime is something new since 1991, when I first went to Copenhagen. Now, there are Arab gangs, run by Palestinians, who clash with Hell's Angels. People didn't seem to want to talk about it very much.

In 1971 some Danish hippies squatted in a section of Copenhagen and declared it to be the "Free State of Christiania." There were abandoned military barracks and other buildings on the site. The Danish government allowed this to take place and declared it to be a "sociological experiment." As long as it went well, Christiania could pursue its independent cultural course. Christianians believe in the use of cannabis, but not in the use of hard drugs. A marijuana and hashish market was set up, just inside a portal of the psychedelic fence that enclosed the community. It was named Pusher Street. In 1994 the experiment was being challenged. Drug dealers from Germany and England had showed up, with the intention of selling hard drugs on Pusher Street—mistakenly thinking that this was an opportune situation for them to pursue their activities. The Christianians were not happy about this circumstance. They invited Copenhagen police to come into the free state and help control the intrusive drug trafficking. On a trip to Copenhagen in 1994, I purchased some hashish, in front of a Danish policewoman, who had a German shepherd dog on a leash. The young woman who sold me the hash explained that the police were there, "to protect us." Shortly after this, some Christianians beat up some foreign drug dealers and tossed them outside the fence. Some Copenhagen police vans were waiting, and the criminals were subsequently deported.

Freetown Christiania, the sociological experiment that is on the edge of the city center, has changed. Marijuana and hashish are still sold there, but the atmosphere has gotten a little grim. It is more like a derelict section of a city, than an alternative community. In 2009 I went there, late one night. I was reminded of the Bowery in New York City, before Soho became gentrified. There were groups of people getting intoxicated, huddled around metal barrels that had fires burning in them. The generation who formed Christiania as a counterculture enclave are older now. The place appeared to be infested with gang members.

One afternoon, I sat in one of the old, quaint bars in Copenhagen. The bar is situated next to the luxurious Hotel D'Angleterre. It faces onto the Kongens Nytorv, an elegant square, not far from the Queen's palace. There were tables set up on the sidewalk, but I preferred the cozy atmosphere inside. As I was sipping a beer, I observed an American couple as they were inquiring about having lunch. They spoke with a waiter, an American student, who was studying in Copenhagen. The tourist couple were concerned about the food. The wife had an allergy to wheat. The specialty of this bar was *smørrebrød:* the open-face sandwiches that Denmark is famous for. When the couple found out that these sandwiches were all that the bar served, in the way of food, they got panicky. The husband began gesticulating with his hands and speaking in a nervous tone of voice, as he said to his wife: "Why don't we go back to the hotel—where it's safe." Perhaps their hotel had a bread-free zone.

At the airport in Copenhagen, just before my departure, I saw someone walking at the bottom of an escalator. He was walking down an escalator that was going up. He was walking just as fast as the escalator was moving—making no progress, until he walked a little quicker. I know how he felt. I was returning to the Costa del Sol, in Spain.

16
A New Decade
(a cautionary rant)

Epithets are given to decades, but many of these nicknames fade from the vernacular. The "Roaring Twenties" still survives in our vocabulary. This decade preceded the Great Depression. During this decade, because of Prohibition, many people were drinking toxic, brain-damaging, illegally-distilled alcohol.

The new decade has yet to rear its ugly head. It's 2010, but the handwriting on the wall is still fuzzy. I take this pessimistic standpoint because of my perception of the progress of the quality of life, over the past five decades. In the United States, the beginning of the 1960s was full of promise. It looked good, at least until the Vietnam War happened. Of course, in 1962 the Cuban Missile Crisis brought America to the brink of WW III, but we didn't know that at that time. In the 1970s there were disturbing foreshadowings—omens. Things looked strange, and commercialization was changing the way of life—noticeably. Then, the 1980s happened. Some people were saying that it was going to go wrong, but it kept going—and here we are.

Decades seem to have their own character. In the 1980s there was a real estate bubble in America. In the 1990s there was a stock market bubble. In the 2000s there was another real estate bubble. Some people made money for nothing. That kind of looting is legal.

New Year's Eves are, for me, problematic—which is to say that I don't expect much from those particular moments in time. The arbitrary expectation! On New Year's Eve of 1989, I was living on the Greek island Santorini. I had been invited to parties, but I decided to stay at home. A little after ten o'clock, I went to bed. Shortly after falling asleep, I was awakened by a mosquito that was buzzing around my head. I turned on the light and waited until the pest was in front of my face. Then, I squashed it—with one clap of my hands. I looked at the clock that was next to my bed. It was midnight. A new decade had just begun. That was one of my better New Year's Eves. I got a good night's sleep. In 1994 I returned to the United States. There, I tried to remain detached from the cultural ethos, as much as possible. After ten years of living in Europe, I found the media noise, to be disturbing.

Socialism is a dirty *word* in the United States. Europeans are perplexed by this. Many Americans associate or equate socialism with communist totalitarianism. Every country in Europe has some sort of socialism. Switzerland has one of the most direct democracies in the world, and it has socialism. Socialism, in the contemporary sense of social democracy, is what a government provides for the citizens of that country, as a guaranteed right: tax funding for social benefits. The word has a complicated history—the ambiguity results from the widespread usage of the word. In the historical context, the word *socialism* has meant a lot of things. In the United States it is now used as a hot-button buzzword in media bombast. What are we really talking about? The talking heads have reduced it to a black-and-white issue. Equating modern social democracy with a communist dictatorship is like throwing out the baby with the bath water.

Flawed is not the word to describe the American medical-care system. The bottom line is that the privatized system of medical insurance in America is not working for the benefit of the people. In the 1990s, in the United States, country doctors were going out of business. The annual cost of medical malpractice insurance was more than they could earn in one year. Now, every doctor has several assistants. A medical group employs a horde of workers, to take care of the paperwork. Many doctors behave like entrepreneurs. What happened to the Hippocratic oath? Doctors in America often scare people (particularly those getting on in years) into thinking that they might have a serious medical problem, advise costly tests (for "peace of mind"), and pass patients off to specialists, their colleagues, who perform the procedures—so that they too, can make a bit of money in the game. Bureaucratically-bloated, for-profit insurance companies take people's money. These corporations make money and raise insurance rates for policyholders. Because of impossible premium prices, people purchase "deductible policies." After paying the insurance company, for nothing, the policyholder still has to pay the medical bills, out of pocket—up to the deductible limit. "Catastrophic" insurance, they call it—meaning, if you need major surgery, become terminally ill, or are hit by a bus and killed—you're covered.

In the early 1990s the Clintons said that they would rectify the problem of medical care in America. It was a campaign promise. A few months into the first term, they said, in effect, that they couldn't do that. Since then it's only gotten worse. What are taxes for? Does the government work for the people, or do the people work for the government. Democracy is supposed to be a government *by* the people and *for* the people. Just to be clear—the Soviet Union had a centrally-organized economy, run by a dictatorship. Even *they* had socialized medicine. Medical care in a modern democracy ought to be a right—not a privilege. It is said that the United States is the richest country in the world. It is the only industrialized country on the planet where the citizens do not have socialized medicine. The members of the United States Congress, however, *do* have socialized medicine.

In 1974 a friend of mine worked as a sales representative for a company that manufactures chest X-ray machines. My friend sold these to hospitals in the United States. At that time it was mandatory to have a chest X-ray before entering a hospital. My friend was curious about this regulation. He found out that insurance companies paid out a lot of money for this test—much more than it actually cost the hospitals. It was a very profitable procedure. My friend quit the job when he couldn't refrain from saying something to his boss.

Extremist ideology is fueling the stasis. Every man for himself. Life is a struggle. The survival of the fittest. Darwinism right-wing style. What has happened to community spirit and the greater good. Turn on the television and listen. It's as though Americans don't know what's in their own best interests. The media has just reported that medical insurance rates in the United States have risen one hundred thirty-one percent, in the last ten years. One CEO of a medical insurance company in the United States is making over thirty-eight million dollars a year. 2020 is coming.

17
Wake Up and Smell the Instant Coffee

There are signs of the Fourth Reich crumbling. I couldn't be happier. Well, I could be—but not until there appears to be some improvement, somewhere in the Western world. Every morning, I stand on the terrace of my flat, in a post-Franco-era apartment block in Spain, waiting to see B-17s flying overhead. Wait a minute—it's 2010. Those planes must be mothballed by now. I am living in the eurozone (the European Union countries that use the euro currency). Europe isn't what it was, twenty-five years ago. Goose-stepping European Union politicians and economists thought that they were going to take over the world, economically speaking, while they instituted the enforcement of things, such as the proper shape of cucumbers. *Heil Brussels!* Their dream to put Europe into a blender and create a Euro-smoothie appears to be faltering. It looks like these European Union leaders got a little too big for their britches.

For decades, countries like Greece and Spain gorged on EU funds. Much of this redistributed wealth went into the pockets of corrupt people. Apparently, the European Union leaders didn't understand the cultures of these countries. It seemed as though "black money" was a term that was unknown to them. Now EU funding is being focused at former Soviet-bloc countries. Greece and Spain are in economic dire straights. Evidently, European bureaucrats need some lessons in knee-bending.

The original, 1980s European Union propaganda was that Europe was to become a third world power: a mediating balance between the two superpowers: the USA and the USSR. "No more wars" was the motto. In 1987 Reagan told Gorbachev to "tear down this wall!" He did—and look what happened. The Berlin Wall came down, the Soviet Union collapsed, and there were the Yugoslav Wars—where UN soldiers from Denmark were forced to watch, and do nothing about, the genocide of elderly people, who were confined to wheelchairs as they were machine-gunned to death. (I have this, from an eyewitness account.) It's like Yogi Berra said: "It's like déjà vu—all over again." One of the consequences of the Yugoslav Wars was that there was a diaspora of Yugoslavians emigrating to more prosperous countries in Europe. This led to calls from the populace of these host countries, for more immigration controls. The more right-wing political parties supported immigration controls, while the more liberal political parties were generally ignoring the issue and claiming political correctness as their excuse for refusing to acknowledge the problem. Inaction, as Yugoslavian gangs erupted in Europe, contributing to a decline in the quality of life in some places.

During the Cold War, America felt threatened by the big, communist political entities: the USSR and Red China. The United States was annoyed with Cuba. Cuba hasn't changed much. Some late-model American automobiles might help, but it could be disadvantageous for tourism there. Now look what has happened. The big, nasty commie-countries have converted to capitalism. Now, they really are screwing up the world. Cuba still annoys America. Many Europeans find it to be a fascinating holiday destination.

The Schengen Area of Europe is a geographical region which has limits on the temporary entry of persons. In the old days, an American only needed to cross a national border occasionally (they were usually close at hand) in order to stay in Europe forever. Now, Americans can only stay in the Schengen Area for three months at a time. Somehow, the Schengen Area extends beyond the European Union. This regulation began creeping onto the scene, about 1998. At present, I have a Schengen visa for Spain. This allows me to travel elsewhere in the Schengen Area, for three months at a time. I might return to the USA—if it weren't for the cost of medical insurance there. On my last trip to America, a German passport-control-freak in Frankfurt questioned the validity of my Spanish visa. I told him that Madrid considered it to be valid and said that I couldn't care less what Berlin thought about it. I wasn't entering Germany—I was on my way to the UNITED STATES. In Germany, they occasionally take the word *control,* a little too seriously.

The widespread verbal abuse of hamburgers is rampant in Europe. After a few decades of listening to this nonsense, it's getting a little boring. I wish that I could get a decent hamburger in Europe. Europeans call the Europeanization of Europe, the "Americanization" of Europe. I believe it's called passing the buck—oh, I mean the euro.

18
Castles and Cathedrals

In the Middle Ages things were pretty clear-cut. There were the kings, who lived in castles, and there was the church, which built cathedrals. The two were in cahoots. Imagine the grandeur of the experience of a cathedral, if you lived in a dirt-floored hut.

Nowadays, the political entities are like the church, and the transnational corporations are like the kings. The one tells you what to believe, and the other one takes your money. Taxes are merely the tithe, although it amounts to more than ten percent. Instead of going to heaven, you get a pension—if you're lucky.

Civilizations construct monuments to glorify themselves. Today, most of the monuments in our civilization are corporate office towers. Most of these monumental office buildings are glass-box high-rises. This style of architecture, which permeates urban centers around the world, was originally called the "International Style." (The idea was that this style of architecture would be applicable anywhere in the world.) This architectural idea is a legacy from the Bauhaus: a school of architecture in pre-Hitler Germany. Hitler drove the Bauhaus out of Germany. They went to Chicago: the home of the first skyscraper boom. The Bauhaus architects collaborated with American architects who had similar ideas. Glass-box buildings are masterpieces of energy inefficiency. They are nightmares to heat and air condition. These edifices stand as monuments to global warming. Mies van der Rohe, a noted member of the Bauhaus, designed the "Barcelona Chair," which is one of the most famous designer chairs in the world. The chair is beautiful to look at, but uncomfortable to sit in.

Germany has been one of the chief architects of the eurozone: the part of the European Union that uses the euro currency. It is apparent now, that they had little understanding of the cultures of Mediterranean Europe. The eurozone appears to have been designed chiefly to facilitate big business. This

European Union design is increasingly having the appearance of a boondoggle. The Europeans fell for it, hook, line, and sinker.

The market economy has been evolving for about two thousand years. A notable attempt to redesign the market economy was the experiment called the USSR, which as we all know, was a dismal failure. Evolution is one thing—revolution is another.

The size of a bureaucracy within a system increases exponentially with the growth of the system. This concept is not unknown to economists. As systems get bigger, middlemen breed like flies. Systems become more cumbersome and unmanageable. The United States is a prime example of this phenomenon—as was the Roman Empire. Smaller systems operate more efficiently. Switzerland and Denmark are admirable models. Europe was composed of small, more manageable national entities. Now, the Eurocrats are trying to make the United States of Europe. Also, it is a generally accepted precept of economy, that when two systems that are at different stages of economic development are integrated, as the one goes up, the other must come down—they meet somewhere in the middle.

The rapid socioeconomic integration of diverse cultures is a dubious idea, at best. In real economic terms, the consequences of the introduction of the euro were that prices more or less doubled in the eurozone. When the euro was introduced into Spain and Greece, prices were rounded off—to about double. While I was in Holland in 2005, I spoke with a Dutch taxi driver. He told me that within three months after the euro was introduced, his income was reduced by fifty percent—for doing the same amount of work. The diminishment of wealth is being caused, in part, by too many fingers in the pie. Wealth is being drained by systems with super-articulated mazes of bureaucracy.

The relationship between the individual and the system, within the wealth-making machinery of the global economy, is becoming less clear-cut all the time. Supporting the system is increasingly stressful and taxing for the individual. Depending on your point of view and your country of residence, systems are either enveloping you or hanging over your head like a ton of bricks. And things are getting more expensive all the time.

19
American Chop Suey

In New England it is called American chop suey. In other parts of America it is called American goulash. When it comes out of a can, it is called macaroni and beef. My mother made this dish frequently—big pots of it. We would eat it for days. It was delicious. This dish has nothing to do with Hungarian goulash or Chinese chop suey. Of course, Chinese chop suey probably has nothing to do with authentic Chinese cuisine, but that's another issue. American chop suey is composed of elbow macaroni that is smothered in a red sauce that is laced with ground beef. It is like spaghetti bolognese, except for the pasta shape. Spaghetti bolognese is only vaguely derived from traditional pasta dishes that are served in Bologna, Italy.

Americans are all mixed up. That is to say, the United States is a melting pot—except that it is not wholly melted. Immigrants who come to America quickly become acculturated. Then they hear the squabbling that takes place among the talking heads that are spouting off in the media. These media spokespersons are paid to cause a ruckus. The implication of this media bombast is that there are lumps and spurious bits in the American alloy, something like baloney, or bologna. Bologna is similar to mortadella, which originated in Bologna, Italy. Choose your side. It's like professional wrestling. Ideologues rant and rave, as they ideologically bash each other over the head and laugh all the way to the bank. I hope, by this time, that Americans know that professional wrestling is fake.

America is the land that produces Apple computers and Boeing aircraft. It is also the country that produces Barbie dolls and neutron bombs. Neutron bombs are an archaeologist's dream. They kill people, but leave buildings intact. The Barbie doll was modeled after a German doll called Bild Lilli, which was first produced in 1955. The German doll was based on a newspaper cartoon character, who was, for lack of a better word, a fashionable slut. The doll was intended to be a joke gift, for adults. The doll became popular with children, who liked to dress it up, with outfits that were sold separately.

America is "the land of opportunity" and "the land of the free." The United States is a country that possesses immense wealth, vast natural resources, and expansive fertile lands. America has a highly-educated population and efficient access to tools and information. America is riddled with outdated infrastructure. The country has an ill-conceived medical-care insurance system, inexcusable poverty, and urban crime rates that make your skin crawl. Where is America going with this? Pharmaceutical *detail men,* corporate drug pushers, provide mind-numbing obfuscations, in the form of ingestible pills, to alleviate the distress that is caused by these circumstances.

I recently heard of a new innovation that originated in America: electricity-free refrigeration. The device looks like an oversized thermos bottle. It was ostensibly designed for use in impoverished, underdeveloped nations, where people live on little more than a dollar a day. The gadget stays cold for twenty-four hours, after having been boiled for half an hour. It costs about forty dollars. In real economic terms, it is like a camping cooler that would cost thousands of dollars in a developed nation. And, a considerable amount of firewood has to be consumed in order to keep a small quantity of food cool, for a short period of time.

I remember a particular episode of "Burns and Allen," the sitcom from the 1950s, starring George Burns and Gracie Allen. George walks into the kitchen and sees Gracie putting water that she has just boiled, into ice-cube trays. He asks her what she is doing. She says she's freezing the boiled water, so that they can have it any time they want, instantly—without having to take the time to boil it.

20
Buying Food

One evening during the early 1990s, I was a guest at a middle-class American dinner table. The hostess knew that I was in the habit of eating fresh vegetables. In her house she usually served canned vegetables. On that day, she bought some fresh vegetables, for the occasion. When we sat down to dinner, her ten-year-old son took a bite of a string bean, made a face, and said, "I don't like these. They're not sweet enough." Canned vegetables in America often contain sugar. In fact, almost anything in a can in America is likely to contain sugar. Her son had grown up eating sugar-sweetened, limp, soggy, cooked-to-death, canned string beans. In my childhood I was fortunate, in culinary terms. My mother and my two grandmothers were all excellent cooks. They used fresh ingredients and cooked from scratch.

My great-uncle had a farm in New Hampshire. In the 1950s, when I was visiting my grandmother, it was a delightful moment when uncle Edgar came to the house, carrying bushels of fresh vegetables from his farm. Sometimes, my grandmother and I would go picking dandelion greens. She would boil the greens. We would top them with a pat of butter, a sprinkle of salt and pepper, and a splash of cider vinegar. Dandelion greens have become a fashionable gourmet food. These days, suburbanites kill the dandelions on their lawns and then pay a premium price for them at the supermarket.

When I was a child, there were vans that drove through the neighborhood, delivering foods. The Cushman's Bakery truck came around a couple of times every week. Their chocolate doughnuts were delicious. Charles' Chips sold metal, airtight containers of potato chips. The milkman put bottles of milk and cream, fresh from the dairy farm, into boxes on backdoor steps. And of course, in the summertime, there were Popsicle trucks that came around every day.

My maternal grandmother and my mother both made homemade doughnuts. They were the best doughnuts that I have ever eaten. Since I have been living in Europe, I have missed Dunkin' Donuts. They are not as good as my mother's, but they're good. Their chocolate doughnuts are delicious—with a cup of hot coffee. A while back, I purchased a chocolate doughnut from a Dunkin' Donuts shop in Malaga, Spain. It was the first time that I saw a Dunkin' Donuts shop in Europe. I had been waiting for some time, to have a chocolate doughnut. The one that I purchased was nothing like the Dunkin' Donuts that are sold in America. It wasn't a doughnut—but it resembled one. The doughnut-shaped thing had a spongy, insubstantial texture. I ate it, but it didn't do the trick.

When I lived on a Greek island, I ate fresh food. Wild greens and mushrooms were picked from the fields, and fresh herbs were gathered from the hills. In some places, almonds and figs could be gathered. The fish that I ate in Greece were caught in the Aegean Sea—the only unpolluted part of the Mediterranean Sea. When I lived on Santorini, I had an excellent butcher. The freshly-ground beef that I bought from him made some of the best hamburgers that I have ever eaten. Every autumn, I bought a whole beef filet from him. I would cut it up into steaks and freeze them—for special occasions or for when I felt like having a steak. One year, when I asked my butcher if he had a filet for me, he said that he would have one, in a week or ten days. Someone that he knew, on another island, was about to slaughter an animal. He would reserve a filet for me. One day, about a week later, he came running out of his shop when he saw me walking through the village. He had my filet. It was one of the most delicious pieces of meat that I have ever eaten.

In New England there are still farm stands that sell freshly-picked produce. These farm stands are usually located next to the driveway that leads to the farmhouse. Outside the city where I was born, there are several fruit farms that sell apples, peaches, pears, and plums—not the industrial-grade fruits more commonly available in supermarkets today, but the old-fashioned varieties.

I love peaches—real peaches. Today, most peaches are hard and dry. They are nothing like the soft, juicy peaches that I remember. About ten years ago, I heard a story about a peach farmer in California. He had been forced to bulldoze his old-fashioned peach trees and replace them with modern hybrids. The wholesalers wouldn't purchase his old peaches. Real peaches are more fragile and bruise easily. They don't ship well. This farmer kept a few of his old trees, to have some real peaches for his family and friends. Nowadays, trying to find a real peach is like trying to find a needle in a haystack.

One of my favorite foods is corn on the cob—*fresh* corn on the cob, bought directly from the farm. The corn should be steamed and eaten within the first few hours after being picked—before the sugar in the corn begins to turn to starch, and the taste and the texture of the corn changes. There are still corn farms in New England, which sell their corn at roadside stands. A tractor, towing a cart, goes back and forth, from the fields to the stand, all day. Different varieties of corn come out at different times during the corn season. Yellow corn comes out first. A little later in the summer, varieties with yellow and white kernels are available. My favorite is called "Silver Queen." It is a late-season corn. The kernels are all white (there is usually a single yellow kernel to be found somewhere on the cob). The pearl-white kernels on Silver Queen have a caviar-like texture—delicate, juicy, and crisp. Yellow kernels are more chewy; they have thicker skins.

In 2001, when I lived in Arizona, most of the produce sold in Tucson supermarkets was from Mexico. The vegetables were fast-grown and almost tasteless. Along with the insipidness, there could sometimes be detected, the faint aroma of urine. I bought my vegetables from a store that sold California produce.

I once bought some fresh strawberries from a supermarket in Andalusia, in Spain. They looked beautiful—deep-red and shiny. When I got home, I popped a strawberry into my mouth. Strawberries are one of my favorite fruits. The fruit had the appearance and texture of a strawberry, but it was almost flavorless. There was a faint taste, that was like that of a synthetically-flavored candy. In the United States, some strawberries are bombarded with radioactive gamma rays before they are sent to market—to kill microbes and prolong the shipping time. Irradiated strawberries take much longer to rot.

Much of the produce that is available in Spain is almost tasteless. All that is left is the look and texture of the vegetables. In 1966 a B-52 bomber, carrying hydrogen bombs, collided with another aircraft during a mid-air refueling over the Mediterranean Sea, just off the province of Almería, in southern Spain. Both planes crashed. The non-nuclear explosives of two of the nuclear bombs detonated, spreading plutonium onto the ground. More than three million pounds of contaminated soil were shipped back to the United States. In 2006 Spain and the United States agreed to a joint effort, to finish the environmental cleanup of the radioactive contamination. There are still traces of radioactivity in the region. Many of the snails in Almería are radioactive. Much of the produce sold in southern Spain is grown in Almería. In 2010 the United States decided that it wouldn't do any more to clean up the residual radioactivity.

As the progress of the world leads us toward buying prepackaged, instant, microwavable, easy-opening, new-and-improved food, I am reminded of a story that my mother never ceased repeating to me, throughout her life. It was 1967. I had taken my girlfriend to meet my mother. My mother was preparing a dinner. There were some potatoes sitting on the counter, waiting to be baked. My girlfriend asked my mother what they were. My mother told her that they were potatoes.

My girlfriend had a look of surprise on her face when she said, "I thought they came out of a box." My girlfriend had only eaten instant, dehydrated potatoes. She had never seen a potato.

21
A Month in Beachwood Canyon
(and the curse of Andy Warhol)

> I love Los Angeles. I love Hollywood. They're beautiful. Everybody's plastic, but I love plastic. I want to be plastic.
> Andy Warhol

In March of 1982, a month after my wife left me, I decided to make a trip, to clear my head. I chose to visit a friend who I had known since architecture school. He lived in Beachwood Canyon, under the *Hollywood* sign. The sign was plainly visible, in its entirety, from the front door of his house.

There was a vaguely unsettling atmosphere of vacuousness in Los Angeles—created by those who produce the archetypes, idols, and icons that are impressed on the world, cinematically. If you arrived there from New York, they automatically assumed that you were an intellectual. In discussions about music, nobody seemed to know what jazz is or was. In those days LA copied New York. I don't know who they copy these days—possibly themselves. Hollywood seems to have become a parody of itself. Many of the ideas that Americans have about themselves and the the ideas that the rest of the world has about Americans emanate from Hollywood, via the productions coming out of there. It's frightening, when you think about it: the connection between the idolization of famous people and the marketing of experiential desires, passing fancies, and models for ways of life. Celebrities have become a sort of faux royalty. Obsession with celebritydom has become a sociological disorder in the modern world.

When I arrived in Los Angeles, my friend picked me up at the airport. He told me that he had to go to a meeting. Meetings are a big thing in LA. "We'll have a meeting" was a popular expression. My friend's meeting was about an MTV video. When we arrived at the recording studio, I sat in a corner of the room where the meeting was taking place, observing the scene. A soft-rock group that had had a couple of big hits in the 1970s was attempting to reinvent itself, with the help of the people at the meeting. In the 1970s soft-rock was in. In the 1980s it was going out. This group was trying to repackage themselves as a hard-rock group. As far as I know, they didn't succeed in this musical transformation. I don't think that they were ever heard from again.

In the middle of their futile effort, a woman came over to me. She asked me who I was and what I was doing there. She seemed a little nervous, as if I were some sort of a spy. I told her that I was a friend of the director. I explained that I had just flown in from the East Coast, to pay him a visit. He had just picked me up from the airport—that's why I was at the meeting.

"You have no connection with *the business?*" she asked me.

"I'm an artist, and I assure you, I have nothing to do with anything whatsoever that's going on in LA," I informed her. She was relieved and went back to the meeting.

The day that I arrived in Los Angeles, John Belushi died. The news of his death spread around Hollywood, like wildfire. He had overdosed on a *speedball:* an injection of a mixture of cocaine and heroin. At that time heroin was a chic drug in Los Angeles. There were luxury cars parked outside methadone treatment centers.

The other gossip-of-the-day was that Johnny Carson had been given a speeding ticket, on La Cienega Boulevard.

One of the complaints circulating around Los Angeles was that bottom-line businessmen were displacing filmmakers, as the producers of movies.

Some mornings, I would walk down the hill, to have breakfast at the Village Coffee Shop, at the bottom of Beachwood Canyon. It was a cozy place to have a leisurely meal. Scrambled eggs, toast, and bacon—with sliced avocado on the side. Native avocados garnished everything in that restaurant. Ten o'clock was a popular breakfast hour. Life was laid-back in LA. What I liked about LA was this: everyone seemed to be enthusiastically engaged in something. What they were doing was something else. Ned Beatty lived across the street from the café. When he came out of his house and got into his Volvo, heads turned, in the café.

One afternoon on this trip, I went with my friend, to Rodeo Drive, that exclusive and snooty shopping strip in Beverly Hills. I wore a custom-made suit, so as not to be locked up, for walking down the street. I wanted to send some chocolates to my estranged wife, who was in New York State. I had crafted a container: a metal canister with a mechanico-erotic ornament attached to the top. It was made with, among other things, an antique drafting compass. We walked into a chocolate shop on Rodeo Drive. After I had examined the chocolates, I told the salesperson to fill the canister with dark-chocolate-covered buttercreams.

His response was: "But I don't know how much chocolate will go into this container."

"It doesn't matter how much it holds," I said. "Fill it and send it to this address."

"But we sell chocolate by the pound. I don't know how much chocolate will fit into the container," he protested.

"I'll pay for whatever it takes, don't worry," I assured him.

This, my explaining and his saying "but," went around several times. Evidently, he couldn't grasp the concept—or perhaps I wasn't hoity-toity enough for him to go into his toady mode. Finally, the owner of the shop came out from the back room, shooed the underling away, and took care of my order.

"Ralph's on Sunset" was a supermarket that was renowned for being weird—particularly late at night. It was open twenty-four hours a day. Johnny Carson used it as a recurring topic, for jokes in his monologues. The night that I went to Ralph's on Sunset, there were disturbingly large numbers of people, wearing overalls and plaid shirts, and affecting good old hillbilly-boy manners. They were "Dukes of Hazzard" wannabes, drifting around the store, pretending to buy food while they waited to be discovered.

One afternoon, I went to a matinee at Mann's Chinese Theatre. During the movie I heard someone talking, in the row of seats behind me. The voice had a disturbingly eerie quality about it. I turned around, to see that it was Tony Perkins, the actor who played Norman Bates, in Hitchcock's movie *Psycho*.

My friend had a guest-pass, for entrance to the Magic Castle: the private club for magicians, that is in Hollywood. One evening, we went to the Magic Castle. After saying "Open Sesame" to a stuffed owl in the entry room, a wall opened up, and we walked inside. There are bars interspersed throughout the club, and there is a formal dining room, where we ate dinner and were served by a Jeeves-like English waiter. In the Magic Castle there is a room for close-up magic, another for parlor magic, and yet another for stage magic. Throughout the night, we were elbow-to-elbow with magicians. It was (and I thought that I would never use this annoyingly mushy expression), *well*, magical.

Andy Warhol predicted that "Everyone will be famous for fifteen minutes." Warhol espoused commerciality, shallowness, and falseness. In the 1960s and 1970s, Warhol was generally regarded with very little esteem, by most artists. He wasn't taken very seriously. Warhol had been a commercial artist. The story goes, that a rich woman told him he should make paintings. Pop Art was in full swing. Andy asked the woman what he should paint. She told him to make a painting of *money*. "Everybody likes money," she said. That's what he did, followed by Campbell's soup cans, et cetera. Warhol rode the wave of Pop Art, to fame and fortune. In the late 1970s, a gallery in New York hired a

Madison Avenue ad agency, in order to make a new, unknown artist instantly famous. It worked. These days, the art world has taken on the character of another fashion industry. Andy Warhol has become a sort of demigod in what is left of the art world. Young artists aspire to his achievement. The quest for instant fame has become installed as a component of popular culture and implanted as a desire in many minds. Grotesque examples of this impulse appear frequently in the media.

22
Ketchup on White Bread
(swallowing the hype)

Popular culture seems to be taking up a larger space in our lives, with every decade that passes—like some invasive weed. The fascination with the television in the 1950s has grown into an obsession with staring at video screens. The allure of the novelty of pushing buttons has led to a compulsion to fidget with them. As the portion of our lives that is taken up by being absorbed in some kind of media interface grows, the real life that is in front of our noses is being supplanted. The increasing significance of the triviality that infiltrates our lives fills the cultural atmosphere with distracting matters of little consequence to our lives and obscures more important things. Thought is being drowned out by the din of media noise.

When I was nineteen, in 1969, I listened to rock and roll music, but I found significance in Thoreau's *Walden*. By 1979, I noticed that, for some teenagers, rock and roll had taken on a much greater significance than it had done for my generation. Popular music had assumed a mentor-like status. Individuals related to one band and often displayed their musical preference on T-shirts that they wore. Imagined philosophical content in the lyrics of the songs was taken as a guide for their lives. In the 1960s, music was a backdrop for our lives—not a portal to a temple inhabited by gurus.

When I lived on Santorini, in the 1980s and early 1990s, I observed a baffling phenomenon. The houses in the village where I lived were perched on top of a cliff, six hundred feet above the Aegean Sea. The view from the terraces of the houses was the most beautiful sight I have ever seen. The houses faced toward the sunset. Tourists would come on a holiday and lie in lounge chairs on their terraces, reading—their noses buried in a summer-reading book.

On one occasion, when I was sitting on the terrace of a restaurant that was owned by a friend, a customer walked onto the terrace, fastidiously and proudly clutching a copy of Marcel Proust's *Swann's Way*. He sat down, ordered his dinner, and proceeded to read. Not to belittle an extraordinary book, but perhaps that wasn't really the time and place to be reading it. The sun was about to set. My friend, the proprietor of the restaurant, came out onto the terrace and sat at my table. He almost never wore shoes and quite often was accompanied by his donkey. Just as the Proust-reader was digging into his dinner, my friend took out a pocketknife and began to cut calluses off the bottom of his feet, while he took in the sunset.

Popular culture is influencing our ways of life and structuring our lives. The ever-changing packages that are being marketed, come and go, as fads, in the merchandizing of lifestyle and popular mythology. What is happening to the quality of life, in the progress of the world? Are the grass roots being smothered under the AstroTurf?

In 1970, when I was at an art school in Providence, Rhode Island, there was a sandwich shop that was popular with students. This deli had an unusual offering on the menu: a ketchup sandwich—at an outrageous price. The sandwich was called "the rip-off." It was a joke. In those days, no one was fool enough to order one.

23
The Sandwich Revisited

The making of a sandwich is an artful process. The same ingredients can result in very different outcomes. A sandwich is dependent on what's in it, the bread that contains it, and how it is made. Taste, texture, and eater-friendliness are important. For me, egg salad on a crispy baguette doesn't work—unless it's an open-face sandwich—otherwise the egg salad squishes out and falls onto the plate, only to be eaten with a fork. It has something to do with the distribution of pressure on the contents of the sandwich, when a bite is taken.

I love sandwiches and I am not above eating fast-food hamburgers—in a pinch. Americans sometimes need to eat a burger—no matter what. But, there are outside limits. I once ordered a hamburger in a restaurant in Gibraltar. It was the single worst hamburger that I have ever tasted in my life. I took one bite and began to gag. It was completely inedible. I paid and walked out of the establishment, but not without leaving a rather loud comment in my wake.

I recently had a Whopper in Spain, in a Burger King on the Costa del Sol. It was the worst Whopper that I have ever eaten. The beef patty was dry and pulpy. The weed-fed beef had been cremated, and the lettuce, tomato, and onion looked as though they had been processed with a sledge hammer. I should have known better.

The best Whopper that I have eaten was in a Burger King in a small town in the Sonoran Desert, in Arizona, somewhere between Phoenix and Tucson. It was late at night. I was returning to Tucson, where I was living. I had spent the day in Phoenix, and on the drive home, I was hungry. When I saw a Burger King sign up ahead, I pulled off the highway at the next exit and found the restaurant. Inside the Burger King, there were several carloads of people, waiting for their food. I gave my order and waited. This Burger King was run by Mexicans. It took what seemed to be a long time, for hamburgers to come out from the kitchen. I remember mumbling something to myself, about *fast* food. But, when I finally got my Whopper and went back to my truck to eat it, I had a surprise. It was delicious—better than any Whopper that I had ever eaten, or have eaten since.

In 2008, on a trip to the United States, I decided to go back to some restaurants that served sandwiches: places where I had eaten, in the past.

On this trip I visited New Haven, Connecticut. I lived there, three times in my life. While wandering around the city, I passed by the infamous Skull and Bones tomb, walking toward Chapel Street. I turned west and walked a couple of blocks, to Howe Street. There had been a Syrian restaurant there, which I had frequented thirty years earlier. The hummus and falafel had been exquisite, and the lamb kebabs had been tender, succulent, and cooked to perfection. And, the atmosphere in the restaurant was very relaxing—usually. I remember one day in 1980, at the time when American diplomats were being held hostage in the American Embassy in Tehran. The Ayatollah Khomeini had come to power. A couple of intoxicated Americans came into the restaurant and accused the proprietors of being Iranians. The owners put their hands into the air and said, "We're not Iranians; we're Syrians!" It was a tense moment. I yelled across the restaurant and informed the intruders that the proprietors were, in fact, Syrians. The two louts grunted and skulked off. I finished my hummus in peace. To my amazement, the restaurant was still there, and the interior was exactly the same as before. The only difference was in the proprietor, who was older—as was I. I glanced nostalgically at the table where I had eaten so many lunches. I then ordered a falafel pocket-pita sandwich, to go. I wanted to continue my trek around my old haunts. The sandwich was the same as before—well-made and delicious. My first bite was a Proustian experience. Even the taste of the tomatoes was the same as I remembered them. They always had a unique taste. I don't know why.

One afternoon on this trip to the United States, I went to a restaurant that serves hamburgers. I hadn't been there in about twenty years. I first went there, thirty-six years earlier. The place was the same, but the hamburgers were slightly different. The shape of the patty had changed. The hamburgers were thicker in the middle and smaller in diameter. The hamburger didn't fill out the toast. The toast kept breaking around the edges of the sandwich. The tomato and onion were cut thick and kept falling out onto the plate. It was an awkward construction, made from the same ingredients. In the past, the hamburgers conformed to the size of the toast, and the thinly sliced onion and tomato seemed to be fused onto the top of the meat patty. The hamburgers almost melted in your mouth. They were, by far, the best hamburgers that I have ever eaten. The restaurant had a homey atmosphere, a homespun elegance. The place now has a touristic atmosphere.

When I was in art school in Providence, Rhode Island, I often ate lunches in a deli, where one could design one's own sandwich. Meats, fish, cheeses, vegetables, spreads, and a variety of breads were available, as the makings. The sandwich-makers were adept at crafting your desired sandwich. I had eaten in this sandwich shop, almost forty years earlier. On this trip, I had a sandwich in this deli. Remarkably, this place too, had the same interior. Apart from the addition of a couple of tables and chairs, the only noticeable difference was the wooden pickle barrel, which now has a plastic liner. I studied the ingredient menus and ordered a sandwich. The sandwiches were made the same way, and the ingredients were the same—except for the bread. Instead of substantial rye bread, the sandwich was made with the kind of soft, mushy bread that is sold in the cheap-bread section of supermarkets in America. The sandwich was delicious, but the bread didn't stand up to the contents. It became soggy, and the sandwich began to fall apart. A chain is no stronger than its weakest link.

In 2009 I visited Copenhagen: my favorite city in Europe. One afternoon, I went to my favorite café in Copenhagen. They served delicious sandwiches. I was looking forward to having a lunch there. I hadn't been there in eleven years. I went in on a Sunday afternoon. The café had the same atmosphere, but I got a shock when I looked at the menu. The sandwiches cost about thirty-five dollars each. It seemed a bit exorbitant. The only person that I saw eating a sandwich was a waitress, who was on her break. The place was empty. In the past the café had been full of people on Sunday afternoons. I drank a couple of beers and soaked up the atmosphere. Then, I went around the corner, to a McDonald's, and ate a McFeast. As far as I know, Scandinavia is the only place where McDonald's serves this particular item on their menu. I do like a good McFeast.

While living on the Costa del Sol, in Spain, I went to a well-known, internationally-conspicuous theme restaurant, in Puerto Banus. I had avoided this event for more than twenty-five years. I had a theory about the T-shirts that had the name of this restaurant plastered on the front, back when I first lived in Europe and began seeing these T-shirts pop up. I always assumed that the individual wearing the shirt lived as far as possible from the locale of the particular restaurant that was emblazoned on the shirt. Shirts for show-offs. Puerto Banus, the port next to Marbella, is the most ridiculously pretentious place that I have ever seen. The food in this theme restaurant was all right, but the prices were a little steep. The portions of meat were absurdly inordinate. A ten-ounce hamburger. Who, in their right mind, wants to eat a ten-ounce hamburger. The picture on the menu put me off having a hamburger. It had indigestion written all over it. It appeared to be made for people with big mouths and the equivalent of seventeen dollars to spend on a hamburger. I partook of a "barbecue" sandwich. I had eaten these sandwiches in Tennessee, back in the 1970s. The sandwich in this theme restaurant was piled high with barbecued pork meat. It was too high to eat—a monument to gluttony. There was twice as much meat as the bun could handle. The sandwich was served with minuscule portions of Boston Baked Beans and coleslaw. Barbecue sauce was mixed in with the meat. When I ate these sandwiches in Tennessee, the sauce was added on top, at the discretion of the consumer.

It was as though they were holding you for ransom, forcing you to pay for twice as much as you wanted—reinforcing the European cliché concerning the obesity of Americans. The items on the menu in this theme restaurant appeared to be myth-reinforcing deformations of American cuisine. While I sat there, attempting to eat my meal, I overheard a Levi-wearing European, making anti-American remarks, as he ate his hamburger. I felt like asking him what he was doing there.

A well-known news magazine that specializes in economic issues uses something that they call the "Big Mac Index," as an economic indicator. It has to do with exchange-rate theory as related to purchasing-power parity. They compare the price of Big Macs in different places in the world. It is a clever statistical device, but is it reflective of real economy? In 1995 I was in Lisbon, Portugal. I was curious about the Big Mac Index. I walked into a McDonald's in the center of Lisbon, with no intention of eating a Big Mac. The restaurant was full of men wearing suits and ties. You don't often see that in America. The price of a Big Mac was ridiculously high—in comparison with America. I walked out of the fast-food restaurant and went to a restaurant that had tables with linen tablecloths and waiters wearing vests. I ordered a hamburger. It was a good-sized and delicious hamburger—and it cost considerably less than a Big Mac in Portugal. The next day, I had a hamburger in a fast-food café in Lisbon. This hamburger cost less than half the price of a Big Mac, although it was equally as big and of comparable quality. In America, Big Macs are one of the cheapest burgers available. In Portugal they were possibly the most expensive hamburger—at the opposite end of the economic spectrum, from where they are positioned in America. Apparently, professional currency traders take notice of the Big Mac Index.

24
Via Media

In America the attractions and distractions of the media show include factual inanity, fatuous substantiality, convoluted clarity, lucid confusion, and focused distortion—all brought to you by squabbling talking heads, as they foment divisiveness and create ideological polarization, through their skewed viewpoints. These professional ideologues have dashboards full of hot buttons to push. Extremism-lite provides an appealing standpoint, for some. The notion of cooperative collaboration toward a goal of the common good seems to be disappearing from the American cultural ideology. The cultural isolationism of the United States is causing a kind of ideological inbreeding. Where do culture-bound Americans go from here? Whatever happened to the middle road?

In Europe the ways of life are changing. Twenty-five years ago, Europe was composed of individual countries with different ways of life. During the last quarter century, Europe has undergone a transformation. The European Union and the euro currency are largely responsible for this change. In the 1980s Europeans were convinced that it was a good idea for Europe to become a third superpower—a mediating power between the United States and the now defunct Soviet Union. The Soviet Union collapsed, but the power of transnational corporations had got its foot firmly planted in the back door of Europe. The euro was to become a currency to rival the dollar. Underdeveloped countries in the European Union were to be brought into socioeconomic parity with the highly-developed industrialized countries. It doesn't seem to be working as planned. Economic redesign is risky business. The Soviet Union was a good example of this. Europeans were swept along in the current of transformation and misled by cockeyed propaganda.

It was Christmas Day, 1979, and I was standing outside the train station in New Haven, Connecticut, waiting for a taxi to take me back to my apartment. I had just come down from Springfield, Massachusetts, my hometown. There was a group of people, in their late teens and early twenties, milling around in front of a shiny, white, unmarked van that was parked in the taxi stand. One of the girls asked me if I needed a ride. She then asked me if I would like to have a Christmas dinner with her and her friends. They were "Moonies." I was sure of it. I asked her if they were, in fact, Moonies. She denied it and explained that they belonged to some *other* group. I had read that Moonies were posing as this other group. A trip to Florida was mentioned. It was very cheap and all-inclusive. It cost a little more than twenty dollars. I was curious. Moonies were recruiting. I looked young for my age. They may have thought that I was about twenty years old and seemingly alone on Christmas Day. It had been reported in the media, that this religious group was using high-pressure recruiting techniques that involved brainwashing and mind control. They advocated an individual's separation from their family, in favor of devotion to Sun Myung Moon and the Unification Church. Also, they insisted that you give them *all* of your money. I decided to accompany them.

Moonies are devotees of the Reverend Sun Myung Moon, the head of the Unification Church. His disciples believe that he is the Messiah: the second coming of Christ. Jesus supposedly came to the reverend, in person, and asked Moon to carry on with his work, which was cut short by his untimely crucifixion. Mr. Moon owns an international media conglomerate.

After a drive across town, the group ushered me into an old house. My bag was taken and placed in a corner of the living room. I sat down on a couch. Young women came over to me and inquired about my well-being, as they stroked my thigh, just above my knee. After a few minutes of this naughty attention, two young men came up to me and informed me that I was to attend a lecture. I was taken upstairs and escorted into a room. There were three folding chairs set up side by side, in front of a blackboard. I was seated in the middle chair. The two escorts seated themselves on either side of me. A minute later, a Korean man came into the room and greeted me. He was the first person I saw in the house, that was over the age of twenty-two. He talked in a monotone while he drew diagrams and wrote words on the blackboard. He was drawing a schema that was meant to explain the cosmos. I payed attention, watching him construct the convoluted chart. When he had finished, I asked him a few questions. I had detected a few flaws in his overview of the universe and had noticed some spurious uses of logic in his conceptual progression. He didn't answer any of the questions or respond to any of the comments. He erased the blackboard and redrew precisely the same thing, as he repeated the same words, over again. The third time around, he decided to give up on me. I clearly wasn't getting the point. The Korean man left the room, and I went back downstairs, with my two shadows. They began to talk about dinner, and the thigh-stroking from the girls began again. I decided that I had to get out of there. I wasn't about to consume anything in that place. A week later, the news media reported that a group of anti-cult specialists had crashed into a Moonie compound in Florida, rescued some bewildered sons and daughters, and brought them back to their families.

The stage is being set. The semiological scenery is falling into place, for the next act of the dog and pony show. Subliminal patterns are morphing into newer forms. Media addicts eagerly await the rise of the curtain. Professional zealots are being attended to in makeup rooms. Media-saturated minds will be swept along by the tides in the media that help determine what is in the public eye.

25
Plating Food

The practice of plating food has gone overboard. Aesthetics are not mutually exclusive to good food, but they can get in the way. Visual appeal is important, but not at the expense of the taste of the food and the eating experience. It can be a daunting task, eating a sculptural arrangement of food. All too frequently, the excessively-ornate architectonic structure, produced by some self-styled artist-chef, needs to be demolished and turned into a nondescript hodgepodge of food before it can be eaten.

This trend in Western cuisine erupted in France in the late 1960s. "Nouvelle cuisine" was a departure from classical haute cuisine. The emphasis, in this way of cooking, was on lighter, more healthy cooking, without so many heavy sauces. There was an emphasis on visual *presentation*. Nouvelle cuisine influenced the development of "fusion cuisine," which began to develop in the 1970s. Fusing different cuisines and increasing the emphasis on plating the food became a trend. This excessively ornamental approach to putting food on a plate was inspired by Japanese cuisine. Delicate arrangements of food are in keeping with the way of eating in Japan. Japanese food is eaten with chopsticks. The chef cuts the food in the kitchen and plates the food in a way that is adapted to the use of chopsticks. Knives and forks are not necessary in Japanese cuisine. In Western cuisines we cut our own food, on the plate. The ornamental plating of Japanese cuisine is appropriate for eating delicate arrangements of food, using chopsticks. In a knife-and-fork culture, this can be an ordeal—an awkward task.

Sandwiches have undoubtedly been eaten since the beginning of bread. A sandwich ought to be able to be eaten without a plate. Sandwiches are hand-held food. The design of a sandwich is as important as the contents that are sandwiched in between the bread. Sandwiches should be handy to eat.

Sandwiches are peculiar in England. The "sandwich" is named after an English earl. The eighteenth-century Earl of Sandwich liked to gamble when he was at his club. Not wanting to take the time to sit down to a meal and not wanting to soil the playing cards with food residue, he had his roast beef brought to him, served between two slices of bread. A sandwich was an ideal solution to facilitate his addiction. For this, they named the sandwich after him. In England, sandwich design is rather perplexing. The English don't seem to grasp the concept of the sandwich. First of all, there is too little in between the bread. They are stingy with the filling. Secondly, they use too much bread. It's as though they got it backwards. In England sandwiches are made from overly-thick slabs of bread or huge rolls. The filling appears to be an afterthought—a garnish. A notable exception to this is the English hamburger. How many times have I seen some Englishman struggling with a hamburger. In England, unmanageable, top-heavy, half-pound hamburgers are quite often dismantled and eaten with a knife and fork. The quality of hamburgers in London is generally deplorable. For the equivalent of ten dollars, one gets an overcooked, dry, pulpy, microwaved lump of meat, that is served cold. The layers of garnish that are shown on the menu are reduced to something that appears to be a photographic imprint on the top of the burger. These "hamburgers" are served by waiters who make the Parisian café waiters of the 1980s look amiable. No amount of ketchup can help.

The "doner kebab" is a particularly egregious example of bad sandwich design. They are a favorite snack for post-pub gobbling in England, easily obtainable in kebab takeaways that are conveniently located anywhere there are pubs. In England, a Turk is given credit for inventing the doner kebab. He is said to have devised the idea for this sandwich in 1971, in Germany. He introduced it to Berlin migrant workers, as a convenient way for them to eat on the run. From there it was passed on to England. I rather imagine that kebabs were eaten prior to 1971. In contrast to most English sandwiches, doner kebabs have too much filling and not enough bread. They are impossible to eat as sandwiches. Diaphanous pita bread is buried beneath a heap of indeterminate meat that is sometimes known as "elephant leg." (Kebab shops, claiming to be *halal,* have been found to be selling pork meat, among other things.) The meat is sliced off a column of meat that is roasting on a rotating vertical spit. The column is made of layers of meat and other spurious animal parts that have been impaled over a skewer. The shreds of meat that are cut off are placed atop a mound of iceberg lettuce that is intermingled with a few bits of indeterminate vegetable matter. Finally, this quasi-esculent pile of culinary debris is crowned with some sauce that is laced with monosodium glutamate and full of saturated fat. Doner kebabs are very popular in England. The National Health Service is concerned.

I recently walked into a kebab shop in Kingston-upon-Thames. I examined the photos of the offerings, as well as the ingredients displayed before me in the vitrine. The price of the kebabs was equivalent to eight dollars apiece.

The proprietor of the shop said, "Can I help you, sir?"

I think he was from Pakistan. I answered, "What are these?"

He replied: "Excuse me, sir. How old are you? These are *kebabs*."

I declined to partake of one. I may have mentioned that I was sixty years old and had eaten *real* kebabs in Istanbul, before he was born—just before I walked out of the shop and went to a McDonald's, for a double cheeseburger—at one quarter the price of the so-called "kebab."

The Italians got the idea for pasta from somewhere. Some say it was from China, while others say that this food form was derived from the Middle East. Noodle-like foods have appeared in many places. It was the Italians who took the fundamental idea and transformed it into *pasta*. They used durum wheat semolina, which produces a noodle that is highly malleable, due to the high gluten content of the wheat. The Italians took the basic idea of noodles and created an elaborate array of delectable pasta forms, with different shapes, textures, and surfaces. Myriad kinds of pasta have been designed, waiting to be married to endless varieties of clinging sauces. Twirling spaghetti is a skill that is easily learned in childhood.

The "pollard" is an apt model to illustrate form and function in design. A pollard is a tree whose upper branches have been cut off. They have been a tradition in Europe since the Middle Ages. Pollarding is a system of pruning that results in a dense growth of shoots. These shoots can then be harvested for fuel and for other woodworking uses. It is an efficient way to produce firewood. The pollard has been reduced to an ornamental vestige of the original design—a residual fashion. These days, in British urban forestry, the justification for pollarding is size management and health and safety concerns. Since when did trees become health hazards? The harvested wood is probably put into a landfill.

26
European Cucumbers

Excessive regulation of trivialities is a penchant of European Union bureaucrats. They like to control things. In the European Union a cucumber cannot be sold as Class One, if it bends more than ten millimeters for each ten centimeters in length. Bent cucumbers are taboo. Is cucumber-measuring a job option in the new Europe? More needless middlemen are taking up space, bleeding wealth out of the system, and installing regulatory nonsense, such as "the bent cucumber rule." They sell something called "European cucumbers" in America. They are straight as a rod and don't taste nearly as good as the fat, bent American cucumbers.

Greece has been brought to the brink of ruin because of the introduction of the euro and the imposition of European Union regulations. Greece is classified by the media as being one of the PIIGS: Portugal, Ireland, Italy, Greece, and Spain—the countries that threaten to bring down the euro currency. They are all known for their endemic corruption. With the coming of the euro, it didn't take too many years before Greece began giving up traditional cultural ways. The lure of the bells and whistles of the modern consumer society led them down the path to this condition. Bank loans proliferated. There was the expectation of more tourism. The Greeks were buying debt along with all the other consumer goods. There is now talk of Greece returning to the drachma.

Greece entered into the European Union in 1981. At that time Greece was a popular destination for travelers. Prices were very cheap, and the experience of the old way of life in the villages was like stepping back in time—like being in a living museum. Now, Greece is like a dilapidated theme park, trying to scrounge up customers to buy outrageously-priced tickets.

The European Union influenced policy in Greece during the 1980s, with the intention of transforming the role of tourism in the economy. Greece decided to attract high-paying tourists who would come to be accommodated for a few days, rather than long-staying travelers who were exploring the culture and staying for months, even years. In the old days, life was good for both Greeks and hard-currency-holding travelers. There was a *freedom* in the way of life. Then, policies were introduced, intended to convert Greece into a place for upmarket tourism. Backpackers were discouraged. Tourists, who were willing to pay more, came to Greece, for "fun in the sun." After the introduction of the euro, prices in Greece skyrocketed. Many travelers chose to go to Turkey. It was much cheaper to travel there. The future of tourism in Greece is now in question, because of "the crisis."

As the charm of Greek villages diminishes, the cost of being there goes up. Prices are ludicrous in Greece. The Greeks are biting their own hands—the hands that *were* feeding themselves. Greece has been transformed, from a paradise-like, antique culture on the edge of Europe, to a depressed backwater of the eurozone.

In January of 1997 I made an exploratory trip to Portugal. A year earlier, I had been in Portugal. On this trip I spent a month living in Tavira, a town on the southern coast. At the beginning and at the end of my stay in Portugal, I spent some days in Lisbon. On my first trip to Portugal, in 1987, Lisbon was an enchanting city. Portugal entered into the European Union in 1986.

On the trip in 1997, I was shocked to find out that prices in Lisbon had doubled in one year. My hotel had doubled the room rates, and my favorite restaurant had doubled the prices on the menu. And this was before the introduction of the euro. They were jumping the gun. At a restaurant in Tavira, where I ate my afternoon meals, I met a couple of Portuguese economists. I asked them what they thought about the coming introduction of a new currency into Portugal. They were all for it. Their education had indoctrinated them to be macroeconomists. They were a bit sketchy about some of the basic precepts of economic thinking, but they were enthusiastic about the future for Portugal, with the coming of the euro.

Evenings in Tavira, I ate my supper in a small taverna that was owned by a friend. A couple of years earlier, he had moved to Tavira because the taverna that he had had in Lisbon became economically unviable. A simple restaurant that served home-cooked food could no longer generate enough revenue to support his family, with the increased cost of living in Lisbon. At that time, many Lisboans were fleeing Lisbon, to live along a strip of commuter rail line that runs out of the city. Industrial-grade, dehumanized apartment complexes lined the train route for thirty kilometers. Real estate values were skyrocketing in Lisbon, and it was becoming economically impossible for many people to live in the city in which they worked. Portuguese were buying Spanish milk because the milk from the local dairy was too expensive.

In the 1990s, industrial pig farms were introduced into Portugal. Portugal was famous for its pork. Many traditional free-range pig farms raised pigs that were fed on roasted potatoes. The pork was delicious. The superimposition of European Union bureaucracy and authority was causing changes in the way of life in Portugal. The industrial-grade pork was less expensive than the artisanal meat, and small farms were being displaced.

In April 2011, Portugal was the third one of the five PIIGS to go down, economically speaking. "United in Diversity" is the motto of the European Union. One wonders if the union will be united in adversity.

27
Ball Games
(myopic worldviews)

When I was a child, I played baseball. In those days, Mickey Mantle was a baseball star and a role model. He played for the New York Yankees. Mickey Mantle was a superstar—before the word *superstar* came into the vernacular. My father bought me baseball cards. My friends and I "flipped" these cards (onto the ground) in a game of gambling, to win cards. In America a "ball game" is synonymous with baseball. It is the quintessential American sport. When a batter steps up to the plate, it is he alone who faces the other team. It is stark individualism in a bat-and-ball sport—in contrast to games of football. Baseball has its roots in England.

    The English like to say that the game of baseball is derived from "rounders," a *schoolgirl's* game. I always make a point of asking the English, how *they* would like to have a ninety mile per hour hardball thrown at their head. On the English side of the pond, they compare baseball to cricket, their bat-and-ball game. Rounders and an early form of baseball were being played in eighteenth-century England. The game of cricket is probably derived from "stoolball," a game that was played by milkmaids. It dates back to the fifteenth century. (The milking stools were the wickets.) Cricket has been played in England since the sixteenth century. By the eighteenth century, cricket was considered to be the national sport of England. How can you compare the view of a scruffy, rectangular patch of dirt on a cricket pitch, with the majestic sight of a baseball diamond. Rounders and an early form of baseball were brought to America by British and Irish immigrants. The modern version developed in the United States. By the late nineteenth century, baseball was considered to be the national sport of America. Stoolball is still being played in some places in England (mostly by women), but (for reasons of health and safety) they must use a tennis ball.

Varieties of competitive games, using hands, feet, and sticks to propel a ball toward a goal have been around for a long time. Hurling is a sport that can be traced back to prehistoric times. Today, it is played chiefly in Ireland. Some form of the game has been played there, for at least two thousand years. The Celts brought the game to the Emerald Isle. Hurling is said to be the fastest field team sport. The game is like ice hockey played on a grassy field, with a baseball. Hurling is remarkably similar to lacrosse, an ancient Native American sport, which dates back to the twelfth century AD.

Association football, also known as "soccer," is the world's most popular sport. A similar game was played in China in the third century BC. In England this sport dates back to the eighth century. In the nineteenth century, rules were formed, to standardize the various forms of this ball game. A folk myth tells of the origins of this sport in England. The young men from one village and the young men from an adjacent village gathered at a midway point between the villages, opposing each other. They kicked a ball back and forth until it ended up inside one of the two villages. The exuberant emotionalism exuded by some football fans in Europe is baffling. For me, watching a game of soccer on TV is like watching someone else play pinball, with a machine that has little men running around inside.

American football is reminiscent of battles in the American Civil War. Two opposing sides line up, opposing each other on the field. The spectators watch from the safety of the sidelines. Football is derived from soccer and rugby. It is said that rugby was developed in 1823, at the Rugby School in England. Someone who was playing association football broke the rules and caught the ball. He then ran toward the opposition goal, clutching the ball.

In the fourth grade I was given the task of making the equipment necessary to play cricket. At that time our class had a practice teacher, who was just out of college. He decided that we should learn something about British culture. He gave me the task of making the equipment necessary to play cricket. I studied the rules of the game and made an improvised cricket bat and two wickets. On the day that we played cricket, I disagreed with the practice teacher, over the rules of the game. He told me to be quiet and made me sit on the sidelines. I wasn't allowed to play with the equipment that I had made.

Ball games are spectacles. For me, watching a live ball game is like going to the opera. I am not particularly interested in what the opera singers are singing, but the overall spectacle is fascinating. Spectator sports provide a metaphorical framework that describes the spirit which motivates the ideas and ideals of a culture *and* a distracting smokescreen that obfuscates cultural reality: a kind of false tribalism. Is the social function of a ball game to foment factionalism or to encourage solidarity? Playing a game is one thing. The view from the sidelines is something else. What is the goal, and what do the goals matter to the cheering bystanders?

28
Fukushima Fallout

One afternoon when I was living in Jimena de la Frontera, a small Spanish town, I met a university student from England. He was majoring in biological sciences and ecology. I mentioned the fact that politicians were talking about the need for more nuclear power. This ecology student said, "It's clean, isn't it." It wasn't a question. It was a dictional tic.

He grew up near to Sellafield, in England. Sellafield is a nuclear complex that is adjacent to the Lake Country tourist region. On the site are reactors for producing electricity and reprocessing facilities for extracting plutonium from spent nuclear fuel. In 1952 some of the plutonium was used to make Britain's first nuclear bomb. Both the plutonium and the waste fissile materials produced in nuclear power plants are intensely radioactive and dangerous beyond any superlative emphasis. Sellafield has been notorious for leaking radioactive materials into the environment, particularly into the Irish Sea. The complex was formerly known as Windscale. The name was changed because of the notoriety. During the summer of 1986, a few months after the explosion of the nuclear reactor at Chernobyl (about the time of the birth of this budding ecologist), a message by British Nuclear Fuels Limited came onto British television, showing an aerial view of an idyllic landscape, accompanied by grandiose symphonic music. The camera glides over a sheep-dotted landscape, arriving at a view of the hyperboloid cooling towers at Sellafield, just as the music reaches a crescendo. The camera zooms to a close-up of a building labeled as the Sellafield Exhibition Center. A blond family, children-in-hand, is shown entering the building, as a narrator invites the television viewer to visit the center—in order to learn about nuclear energy. Greenpeace attempted to put a message onto British television, offering another view of nuclear energy, but they were denied access to airtime because their message was "of a political nature." At that time, restaurant menus in Ireland often indicated that the fish being served were caught off the *west* coast of that country.

I said that the critical problem was the disposal of the lethal waste, for thousands of years—not whether or not the power plants can be operated safely. His comment was: "I'm not going to be around forever, am I? Let's use it while we've got it." An exemplification of fuzzy logic.

One afternoon when I was in prep school, I was part of a team that blew a hole in one of the clay tennis courts on the campus. When we were done, there was a wok-sized, pothole-shaped crater in center court. Our intention was to see something on a larger scale than we had previously experienced it. Metallic sodium is a volatile metal. It is stored in oil because exposure to air causes it to incinerate spontaneously. Immersion in water causes it to explode. In chemistry class the master dropped a tiny piece of sodium into a large beaker that was filled with water. After a couple of seconds of hissing and smoking, it went off like a firecracker. The piece that he used was about one eighth the size of a green pea. We stole a piece of sodium the size of a golf ball. The sodium was stored in a glass jar that was kept in a locked room next to the chemistry lab. One of the team knew how to pick locks. I was the brains of the operation. A jock was doing the lifting. I made sure that he used tongs. After we stole the metal, we ran out of the science building. The wrestling star and football quarterback lobbed the lump of sodium over the fence, into the middle of a puddle of water in the center of the tennis court. A plume of smoke poured out from the sodium. Then, there was an explosion. A ball of flame the size of a basketball was the visual effect. We dispersed, rather rapidly. Nothing was ever said about it.

I happened to be on a flight from Athens to Paris, at the exact moment that the nuclear power plant at Chernobyl blew up. News of this event appeared in the media, three days later. This was before the Internet. I was in France when it was announced that "radioactive snow" would be falling down for a few days. One day during the snowstorm, I ate some Bélon oysters in a seafood restaurant on the island Belle-Île.

Twenty-five years after the disaster at Chernobyl, there was a disaster at Fukushima, in Japan. It was the result of an earthquake, not the result of slipshod communist technology. Nuclear power plants in earthquake zones are supposed to be "earthquake-resistant." Earthquake-proof would be better, if that is possible. Japan is in a major earthquake zone. Fukushima stands as an example of kamikaze economic development.

The first Earth Day was in 1970. It was a radical event. A few years later, Earth Day was being sponsored by chemical companies. In England, Earth Day 2011 was overshadowed in the media, by Easter, a Royal wedding, the assassination of Osama Bin Laden, and unusually sunny and warm weather. Earth Day has fizzled out as a cultural manifestation. Ecotourism has gone awry. Chernobyl sightseeing tours are a new tourist attraction in Europe.

29
Mothers and Mockingbirds

Mockingbirds mimic the songs of other birds and the sounds of insects and amphibians. When they sing their complex songs, it sounds as though there is a group of different birds singing in sequence. Mockingbirds that live in variable, more difficult climates sing more elaborate songs. These birds can distinguish, in a crowd of people, an individual human intruder who has molested their nest. Mockingbirds attack intruders on their territory.

Perhaps that explains why flamenco music is so popular in Spain. This music is essentially an unpleasant sounding, wailing and whining about life. In Spain, men often live with their mothers, until middle age. Their mothers tend to their rooms, as though their sons were still children.

When I was a child, I spent parts of my summers, staying with my maternal grandmother, who lived in an old railroad station in Jefferson, New Hampshire. My mother grew up in that house. Its only heat was a large, wood-fired, cast-iron stove in the kitchen. There was always a copper kettle on the back of the stove. My grandmother drank her tea in large teacups. These oversized cups are called "pots," in Yorkshire, England. The kitchen window of the train station overlooked Mount Washington, the tallest mountain in the Northeastern United States. The waiting room of the station was my grandmother's bedroom. It was a large and lofty room. The walls of this room were made of oak tongue-and-groove paneling. Around this room there were many cabinets and chests of drawers, which contained curiosities and mementos. My grandmother once gave me a milk-glass egg. These were placed into the nests in chicken coops, to induce chickens to lay eggs. Apparently, chickens are more inclined to lay eggs, if they think they have already laid one.

In 1956, when I was six, my parents were divorced. After that, I lived with my mother. I was a latchkey child. When we first moved into our house, which was in a tract-house development, I told the other kids, that my father was a traveling salesman. I was embarrassed that there was no father in the house. My mother told me that I was now "the man of the house." She told me that I had responsibilities. I had to empty the wastebaskets; take the trash barrels down to the street every week, on trash-pickup day; cook some meals; dust and vacuum sometimes; and mow the lawn every week. I got fifty cents a week allowance for these chores. In those days a candy bar cost a nickel and comic books cost ten cents. I began cooking at age eight. The first meal that I learned to cook was marinated, breaded, baked chicken; and scalloped potatoes. My first attempt to make pancakes was a fiasco. I was alone in the house. I read the recipe in a cookbook. I didn't grasp the idea that it was necessary to oil the pan, each time a new batch of pancakes was put onto the griddle. The second batch quickly began to burn, and the resulting smoke began to circulate around the house. I panicked and dashed next door, to get our neighbor, Mrs. McCabe. She came to rescue me. She was always available, if I needed help. When I was home from school, sick, she would come over a few times every day, to look in on me. After Mrs. McCabe and I had opened all the windows in the house, she explained to me about the necessity of re-oiling the griddle.

A couple of years after my mother divorced my father, she hiked over the Presidential Range, in the White Mountains, in New Hampshire. She came back from the trek with a backpack full of rocks that she had collected. She knew that I was interested in rocks and minerals. I had a book on that subject. Shortly after her trek, we went to a sale of used furniture. She bought a huge (it was about eight feet long) fall-front desk and put it into the basement of the house, for me to use. It had a couple of dozen drawers in the bottom and three desktops, which when folded down, revealed numerous shelves and pigeonholes. I used this desk for making models and for storing my collections of things, including my rock collection.

This same year, I made a fence, next to my mother's house. Someone loaned me a posthole digger. It looked like two skinny shovels that were attached together with a hinge. I dug the postholes, put creosote onto the bottom of the posts, and set them into the ground. After I nailed on the horizontal boards, I painted the fence white.

When I was ten, my mother bought half-ownership of a twenty-six foot cabin cruiser. It was an old boat, built in 1947, and it had to be restored a bit. The boat had a steel hull. The only other steel-hulled cabin cruiser produced at that time was a yacht. The boat was a Steelcraft, built by a company that made, among other things, bows and sterns for submarines. I learned to pilot the boat and to navigate, in rivers on the coast of Connecticut and on Long Island Sound. "Red-right-return" is the motto for river navigation. Red buoys on the right—black buoys on the left—when going upriver.

Quite often, I was allowed to skip school on Mondays, after we had been on the boat for the weekend and got back home late Sunday night. Living on a boat, one quickly adapts to the rocking motion. Returning to land, after a couple of days of living with sea legs, one has the sensation of the earth rocking back and forth—for a brief period, until one adapts again, to land legs.

One afternoon when I was piloting the boat on the Thames River, in Connecticut, I saw some unusual turbulence in the water up ahead. I was heading toward Long Island Sound. I backed off the throttle because I didn't know what was up ahead. All the adults were in the cabin. I was alone on deck. Suddenly, a submarine surfaced, not more than a hundred yards up ahead. There was a submarine base, further up the river. There were some good waves to play with, in the wake of the submarine. I throttled up, and the adults came out of the cabin, to see what was going on. Many years later, I saw this same cabin cruiser, in a dump in my hometown. It still had the name painted on the stern: Full House.

The same year that I went through the wake of a submarine, my mother let me drive her 1960 Studebaker Lark, when she took me up to New Hampshire, to spend a month with my grandmother. The train station was on a quiet country road. I was eleven years old.

In 1962 I went for a month, to a summer camp in Maine. I learned to do many new things at this camp. One day, I signed up for a mountain climb. I was the youngest camper in the group. We climbed Mount Washington and camped near to the top. The next day, we went to the summit, which is 6288 feet above sea level. After spending some time at the top, we hiked back down the mountain, got on the bus, and went back to camp. I was tired, that day, and I hadn't been hauling around a bunch of rocks in my pack.

In 1965 my mother rather abruptly sent me to a New England prep school. The school system in my hometown was not particularly good. My father had to pay for this school. I wasn't very happy about this turn of events, but I realized that I was going to get a good education. I was homesick, the first year that I attended this boarding school. The rigorousness of the school taught me some self-discipline.

My mother died in 1997. In the last months of her life, her medication cost more than one thousand dollars per month. Her Social Security paid a little over eight hundred dollars per month. Medicare paid nothing for medication. Pharmaceuticals in the United States cost many times more than in other industrialized countries, because of lobbyists and the Congress of the United States. There were no supplementary insurance policies available to help. There were no options, except to pay. My mother got her medication before she died, but at the end of her life, she was very disillusioned. How does that work? My mother had worked all her life.

In 2008, on a trip to the United States, I briefly visited my old prep school, Williston Academy. A couple of years after my graduation, the school merged with a private girl's school and became coeducational. Just my luck. It is now called the Williston-Northampton School.

On this visit, I wandered around the campus, thinking about the times that I had spent there. I wondered if there would be any problem with security. It was late in the evening. There was no problem. I came upon a couple of coeds and identified myself as an alumnus from the class of 1968. I asked them if they were getting a good education at that school. "Yeah," they both said, with gleams in their eyes.

During the last years of my mother's life, there was a mockingbird that nested outside her house. It came back, every spring. There were a couple of crab-apple trees in the yard. Mockingbirds are fruit-eaters. The mockingbird serenaded the house, singing a chain of songs and sounds that it had acquired in its life. It sometimes sang during the night, outside the window of the bedroom where I slept, when I was there. There are things in life that make little sense at the time, but later in life, with a bit of wisdom, make quite a bit of sense.

30
Glimpses of a Child's World

My first electric train was a 1940s vintage, Lionel "O" gauge. I got this for Christmas in 1954. The steam locomotive blew smoke out of its stack, and it could whistle. The logs stacked in the log car could be dumped out, with the press of a button. The train set had belonged to my father's boss's son, who had outgrown it.

My parents were divorced in 1956. I ended up living with my mother. On Thursday nights I had dinner with my father, usually in a restaurant. Every summer, my father and I went to Cape Cod together. On the nights that we had dinner together, my dad sometimes stopped to fill up his car with gasoline. He always went to the same gas station: Murphy's. Murphy always waited on my father. He didn't leave the job for one of the young guys who worked for him. When he saw my father pull up, Murphy would walk out of the station and come over to the car. He had a deep, gravelly voice, and he always wore a smile on his face when he greeted my father.

"How are ya doing Al?"

"All right, Murph. How are you?"

Murphy pumped the gas, washed the windshield, and if my father thought it was necessary, checked the oil. In those days gas stations were called "service stations."

In 1956 I went with my father, to an open house and air show at the Strategic Air Command base that was near to my hometown. I sat in the cockpit of a B-36 "Peacemaker." It was a huge airplane—the largest mass-produced piston-engine aircraft ever built. The B-36 had the longest wingspan of any combat aircraft ever built. It was the first intercontinental strategic bomber. The plane was unusual-looking. This airplane had a pusher configuration. There were three propellers on the trailing edge of each wing. There was also a pair of jet engines at the end of each wing. The plane had ten engines in all. At the back of the plane, there was a pressurized rear-crew compartment, with bunks and a galley. There was a pressurized tunnel through the bomb bay, that connected the flight deck with the crew compartment. A wheeled trolley ran through the tunnel, for moving between the two ends of the aircraft. The trolley was pulled along with a rope. I wanted to pull myself down the tunnel that connected the two compartments, but I don't think that that was allowed. Later in the day, I stood beside my father on the side of the runway, to watch a B-52 Stratofortress take off. This plane had been introduced in 1955. It was very loud. B-52s have eight jet engines.

One week, when I was about seven, my father brought me a model stage coach, which he had made out of shirt cardboard. It had rolling wheels, which were mounted on axles and attached to cardboard leaf springs. Shirt cardboards were ideal to use for craft projects. They were stiff and had a smooth, white surface on one side. My father had a lot of white shirts washed and pressed at the cleaners, and he was adept at bricolage. "Westerns" were very popular on TV and in the movies. This same year, my father took me on my first trip to New York City. We went up to the top of the Empire State Building. At that time it was the tallest building in the world.

When I was eight, my mother bought me a baseball glove. It wasn't a real baseball glove. It was a toy glove. It wouldn't fold. It was like a clown's glove. It would never catch a baseball. My mother didn't know any better. When my father saw the glove, I may have pleaded a little. The next week, he brought me a proper Spalding fielder's glove. My mother was a little peeved, but what are you going to do.

In 1959, when I was nine, my father gave me his first-edition copy of *We*, the book that Charles Lindbergh wrote about his famous flight. My father told me that he had seen the *Spirit of St. Louis* flying overhead, in 1927—when *he* was nine years old. The book was a little dry, but fascinating—it was true.

That year, I made a diorama for school. I decided to make a moonscape. I mixed some flour, water, and a little salt together and placed the doughy concoction onto a piece of cardboard. I glued a piece of string onto a golf ball and dropped it onto the unset mixture, pulling it up quickly, after it impacted the soft dough. This technique produced realistic looking craters, including the peak spiking out of the middle. I placed this lunar surface into a cardboard box and made the backdrop: black construction paper with white dots on it. The week that I made this, my father brought me a small present when he came to pick me up for dinner. It was a tiny, carved balsa-wood rocket, with detailed fins. We placed it into the diorama. The surface had dried. The year before, the United States had launched its first rocket into outer space and put a satellite into orbit. The "Space Race" was on.

In 1959, when I began reading Tom Swift Jr. books, Tom had just invented his Electronic Retroscope. He already had his Flying Lab, his Jetmarine, his Rocket Ship, and his Outpost in Space—among other inventions. That year, the B-36 bomber was officially retired. It was made obsolete by the B-52, which has a cruising speed that is more than double that of the B-36.

The first X-15 flew in 1959. The X-15 was a rocket-powered aircraft that was launched from the wing of a B-52. The X-15 was attached to the underside of the wing and carried aloft. At the right altitude it detached from the B-52 and flew off to the edge of outer space. It could fly up to 4520 miles per hour, and up to an altitude of 67 miles. The X-15 holds the record for the fastest speed ever reached by a manned aircraft. I made a plastic model of one.

When I was ten, my father sometimes took me to the computer of the company where he worked. I played with the key-punch machines and the punched-card sorting machines. I encoded the names of girls that I knew, onto the cards, before we placed them into the sorting machine. The IBM computer equipment was housed in a building that was bigger than my father's house.

This same year, at the open house of the Strategic Air Command base that was near to my hometown, I watched the low-level flyover of a B-58 Hustler. The B-58 was the first operational supersonic jet bomber. It had delta wings and was capable of making a sonic boom. It could fly twice as fast as a B-52.

In 2008 I went to a birthday party that was given for a young friend of mine. It was her fourth birthday. I hadn't missed one. The party was taking place on the grounds of a mansion on the coast of Spain. I walked out of my house in the town where I was living and went down to the taxi stand on the main square of the town. There were no taxis. I walked along, thinking that I might find a taxi further down the street. There were none. I saw a Lay's Potato Chip truck that was parked in front of a shop, making a delivery. I approached the driver and asked him how much he wanted, to drive me to the mansion, which was about twenty miles away. He wanted one hundred and fifty euros. I muttered something. The driver then went into a video-rental store and spoke with the proprietor. The proprietor came out from the shop, closed and locked the door to the store, and walked over to me. He offered to take me right to the gate of the mansion. I gave the Lay's Potato Chip man, one hundred and fifty euros. After I got inside the gate of the mansion, someone volunteered to paint my face. Blue fireworks were painted onto my face. I then walked off to find my friend. She was on a tour, led by a nanny. A route of events had been planned. There was a miniature disco, a throne room, and other stage sets set up on the grounds of the mansion. I found her, just as a group of children were dumping fake Barbie dolls at her feet. She was sitting on a throne. There was a pile of these knock-off Barbies lying at her feet. She wasn't impressed.

She had one of these toys given to her every day of her life. I followed the herd of children as they followed my friend and her guardian to the next stage of her birthday tour. At the next position she was seated on another chair, and the children began placing more cheap toys at her feet. She was bored. I looked around at the ground. There were balloons and vials of glitter littering the grass. I picked up a blue balloon and blew it up. It was a large balloon. I held it up in front of her face and let go of it. The balloon took off like a rocket, swirled around in front of her face, and then took off upwards, looping around a couple of times before fizzling out and dropping to the Earth. She stood up, clapped her hands, and laughed. After that, she was led to the next event on the planned tour. In the middle of the walk, she stopped and looked up at me. I had picked up a plastic vial of green glitter. I held it concealed in my hand. At a moment when she glanced down at the ground, I raised my hand over my head, uncapped the vial, and dumped the glitter. By the time she looked up, the vial and cap had been tossed onto the ground on one side of me. She looked up to see a flurry of glitter snowing down in between us. She sat down on the ground and began to pick the glitter off the grass, putting it into her palm. I sat down in front of her and helped her. The nanny took her hand and tried to pull her toward the next event. She shook her head and stubbornly said *no*. The nanny said, "Gregorio is your friend, no?" My friend nodded her head. Later that day, in another place, at another event, I broke one thousand plates in the street of a town in Andalusia. The next week, I found myself banging on the side of the same Lay's Potato Chip truck, demanding a free bag of potato chips. The driver told me to come into the truck and help myself. I did.

One of the best toys that I ever had was a house that was made out of a corrugated-cardboard refrigerator carton.

31
The Crisis of Individual and System

There was a black African wandering around the halls of the dormitory, looking slightly confused and sticking out like a sore thumb. It was the first week of my first year at prep school. The year was 1965. I was homesick. He was the son of an African king. He appeared to be searching for something when he walked over to me in the hallway of the dormitory and asked, "When is the first cocktail party?" Evidently, he had been grossly misinformed as to what a New England prep school is.

"Cocktail parties! There are no cocktail parties. We aren't allowed to drink alcohol," I informed him. He had a shocked look on his face as he turned around and walked away. The following day, he went to a Chevrolet dealership, bought a Corvette, and disappeared. That was the last thing that I heard about him. I envied him. I was in for the long haul.

What is going on in the world in which we live? Is the world your oyster? These days, the oyster is to be found mainly in the marketplace. How much can you afford? Debt will allow you to have more. Living is being reduced to the act of accumulating material culture and experiences. It is a pay-as-you-go life in the consumer society, and the prices are going up. Life is divided between the home, the workplace, and the marketplace. What kind of a life are you going to buy today? The industrialized world revolves around the marketing of life—subject to availability in the marketplace. Experience is a purchasable commodity. Prepackaged lifestyles come in an array of appealing variations. New styles come hot on the heels of the soon-to-be old fashioned. In order to insure economic stability, governments prop up the largest economic units: the transnational corporations that concoct the ephemerally fashionable world that we inhabit. The corporations, in turn, promote a gluttony of consumption in order to profit from it and keep the economic machine going.

Individuals are jaded by excesses of vapid superfluity. Appreciation of the small things in life is being drowned out. There is little time for stopping and flower-smelling. We're on the run. The dilemma of modern man is the choice between "the simple life" and full participation in the rigorous economic rigmarole. The quiet middle road is being torn up, to make way for a busy toll road. Ways of life are being blindsided by progress. The boundaries of life are being delineated by *the System*. The simple life is increasingly inaccessible, as the prerequisites for existence in the consumer society become more and more demanding. The masses evidently can't see the handwriting on the wall in the ocean of media-generated noise. Many are saying that progress is leading us toward an unsustainable culture. In a world of supposed democracies, who is determining the course of progress? Is *democracy* being reduced to a figure of speech? Of course, if you think like Aristotle, you wouldn't trust the average person. The condition of the modern world is up in the air, perched precariously on the brink of economic calamity—or as many pundits put it: at the advent of a glorious future. It remains to be seen. The direction of progress is in doubt. As the world lunges toward unsustainable progress, is the world your oyster? Perhaps, the oyster is morphing into a rattlesnake. Don't worry—it will taste like chicken.

32
The Dehumanization of Technology
(wright and wrong)

Back in the 1980s, when I was living in a village on a Greek island, a Frenchman explained to me that *technology* is only computers and things associated with computers. I pointed out that the word *technology* is an ancient Greek word—and the ancient Greeks didn't have computers. No, I was wrong—the Frenchman informed me. Technology is *only* computers—*they* had told him that in France. I had to get up and leave the table. I couldn't take any more of it. This conversation took place in a taverna. I went home and continued my study of archaeology. Technology is what we use to make things—with the help of our opposable thumbs: man-made processes that produce material culture.

Contrary to popular belief, Thomas Crapper did not invent the flush toilet. Nor did his name become a euphemism for excrement. His surname was coincidentally eponymous. The word *crap* goes back to the Middle Ages. The flush toilet had been in development since prehistoric times. Mr. Crapper did, however, popularize the use of the toilet in the late nineteenth century. He also made some improvements in the device. The flush toilet was a product of technology, whose time had come.

In the late eighteenth century Count Rumford (Benjamin Thompson) designed and made a more efficient fireplace. It radiated heat more effectively than conventional fireplaces. In a conventional fireplace most of the heat goes up the chimney. Count Rumford was born in Massachusetts, but he was a Loyalist. When the Revolutionary War started, he abandoned his wife and went to work with the British. At the conclusion of the war, he moved to London. He is buried in Paris. The Rumford Fireplace became popular in America and in England. Many conventional fireplaces in New England were "Rumfordized." Oddly, there is little evidence of this technology, left in the world.

It has nearly disappeared from the scene, unlike the flush toilet. The advent of central heating may have had something to do with this cultural amnesia.

What are we making—and why? The artifacts that are produced are inextricably linked to the course of progress that is being pursued. They constitute part of the structure of our way of life. Do these technological innovations enhance and enrich our lives, or do they trap us in the rat race—forever indebted and indentured to the system which envelops us.

One of the stated justifications for the Space Race was that technological seepage would lead to products being developed that would indirectly benefit our lives—by-products of space technology. Of course, the Space Race was linked to the Cold War. There is only a slight difference between a manned rocketship and an intercontinental ballistic missile.

What is *the real cost of technology?* I have seen proposals for urban skyscraper farms. How much are *those* vegetables going to cost, considering the value of urban real estate? What happened to crossing the road directly, rather than heading in the wrong direction and going around the world in order to get to where you're going—paying tolls along the way. How much wealth is expended in order to produce the artifacts that make up the artificial world around us? What does the Space Race have to do with the rat race? What are these *things* to us? Are they monuments to inspire awe or improvements in the quality of our lives? You would think that a country who put a man on the Moon ought to be able to make better houses. The United States has put a man on the Moon, but the quality of house construction in America is atrocious. Average house sizes have more than doubled in America during the last sixty years. Flimsy, matchstick McMansions, with wolves puffing at their doors, are all the rage with the affluent.

According to my parents, the first full sentence that I ever spoke was: "I want some *muckiss* on the *zoo-zoo*." There was a radio in our living room. It was from the 1930s and was about the size of four microwave ovens. When I twirled the tuner around when the radio was set on the shortwave band, it made a *zoo, zoo, zoo-ooo* sound. *Muckiss* meant music. Before we had a television, this old radio was a presence in the living room. In 1952 we bought a TV. The television usurped the position of the radio in the living room. The radio had had a far less intrusive presence than the television.

The "transistor" was introduced in 1947. The transistor would replace vacuum tubes in electronic devices—a stage in the development of miniaturization in electronics. In 1954 portable transistor radios came on the market. The initial offerings were expensive. They were a milestone in the development of personal appliances. In 1957 transistor radios began to be mass-marketed, by Sony. In 1960, when I was ten years old, transistor radios became a fad. Every kid had one. Three transistors or five. Mine had five. The radios were about the size of two packs of cigarettes. They were very popular with young teens. It was *cool* to be seen walking down the sidewalk, with a radio held up against your ear—a reaction to the poor sound quality of the speaker. This short-lived fad was the beginning of a trend. In 1979 the Sony Walkman came on the market—a cassette player married to a radio. The Discman came on the market in 1984. By that time, cassette Walkmans had become traveling gear, de rigueur. In the 1990s the MP3 player was introduced. More miniaturized interface technology is a trend.

When the focus of attention is directed at the ocean of cyberspace, cerebral activity tends to become exteriorized into an electronic device. It is "bread and circuses" in continuum, in the arena created through microcircuitry and display screens. Individuals are becoming addicted to the babel emanating from cyberspace. As interface technology proliferates, individuals are spending more and more time being absorbed in something emanating from an electronic device. Immersion in cyberscapes has become a popular avocation. Attention spans are being shortened, and social connections are being diminished. Some individuals are aspiring to be a node in the network of oblivion, drifting like rudderless boats, addicted to the road trip along the information superhighway that runs through the middle of the rat race—spam billboards and all.

Cheese puffs are a curious product—inflated Mylar bags, half full of highly-aerated, styrofoam-like, worm-shaped snacks: cheese-flavored air, with a crispy texture. A cheesy sensation. There's almost nothing to them.

33
Plan B
(the handwriting on the wall)

Thomas Hobson owned a livery stable in Cambridge, England. He lived from 1544 to 1631. In his stable, he gave customers a choice of renting the horse in the first stall, or renting no horse at all. This prevented his best horses from being overworked. The expression "Hobson's choice" refers to a free choice with only one option. The Ford Model T was available in any color, so long as it was black.

Humanity is approaching the condition of being on the horns of the dilemma of Hobson's choice. Take it or leave it. There is a kaleidoscopic profusion of various style modes, if you choose to take it and function as an ancillary of a giant system that appears to be running amok.

What are the alternatives? The top-heavy superstructure of the modern world is becoming increasingly costly to maintain. The global economy is supported by an osteoporotic financial spine. Are individuals, satiated with superfluity, being lulled into being realists, accepting things as they are, or are there strains of idealism that might lead to improvements being made in the condition of human culture. The future of our standards of living is in question. Are we going to just glibly complain, or are we going to do something to change the headlong course of progress. The overhead costs are increasing in the modern world.

Flash Gordon was a science-fiction comic strip that was started in 1934. It was created to compete with the already popular *Buck Rogers* comic strip. Flash was a Yale graduate and a polo player. Ming the Merciless was a tyrant on the planet Mongo. Ming was bombarding the Earth, with fiery meteorites. Flash flew in a rocketship, to the planet Mongo, to sort things out.

Buck Rogers was working for the American Radioactive Gas Corporation in 1927, when he was accidently exposed to some radioactive gas. Buck fell into a state of suspended animation. He awoke in the year 2419, after sleeping for 492 years—something like a science-fiction version of Rip Van Winkle. After his awakening, he discovered that North America was ruled by the Hans, who lived in fifteen great cities. The Hans, because of their advanced technology, had no need for slave labor. The masses of people were left to fend for themselves, in the forests and mountains of North America.

Some people have been making forays into "the simple life." Simplicity is complicated in the modern world. Advocates would say that the experience of life is richer in the simple life, with fewer mind-numbing distractions and addictions, and far fewer monetary expenditures. It is a more natural life. Urban centers around the world are being transformed into theme-park-like attractions. Cultural homogenization is taking place. As human culture becomes more and more commercialized, individuals are paying for more and more things. A downsizing of standards of living is occurring. The social fabric is being stretched thin. What room is there for community spirit, in a dog-eat-dog world? What possibilities exist, that would allow the individual to diverge from the mainstream, in pursuit of a more simple life?

In the mid nineteenth century Henry David Thoreau said that the vital necessities of life are Food, Shelter, Clothing, and Fuel. He examined the lengths that individuals went to in order to acquire the things that are needed for subsistence. He was reacting to the cultural transformations that were taking place as the result of the Industrial Revolution. Things have only gotten more complicated since that time. These days, in the case of procuring strawberries, a blast of gamma rays may be involved. There are a lot of value-added factors, raising the prices in the marketplace.

The domestic vehicle is the fundamental force that drives the massive machinery of the global economy. The consumption of products and services fuels the system. In the maintenance of household culture, people are, paradoxically, working to save time. This results in households eating instant microwaveable meals, as if they were living in a space capsule, rather than taking the time to cook a meal from scratch—a much less expensive and gastronomically more rewarding way of utilizing a kitchen. Is the process of consumption enhancing or encumbering lives? In the growth of economy, individuals are expected to run faster and faster, following hot on the heels of incipiently-outdated fashion in consumer goods and services—led on by the onslaught of marketing that floods the cultural environment.

I have seen the demise of the soda fountain. The final extinction of soda fountains took place in the early 1970s, the decade that saw a significant ratcheting up of commercialization in the culture of the United States. By the early twentieth century, soda fountains were common in drug stores. Soda fountains sold effervescent beverages and ice cream. Often, these bubbly elixirs contained cocaine and caffeine. In 1914 the "Harrison Narcotics Tax Act" effectively prohibited the sale of cocaine and opiates, over the counter. Soda fountains began to dispense "soft drinks."

When I was a child, in the 1950s, I used to pedal my bicycle to Normans' Pharmacy. (Two Normans owned it.) In those days pharmacists owned drugstores, and pharmacies had soda fountains. I got fifty cents a week for an allowance—for doing chores around the house. At that time candy bars cost five cents and comic books cost ten cents. A Coke at a soda fountain cost ten cents. Normans' Pharmacy was located in a small shopping plaza that was not too far from my house. It was in a strip mall that also had a First National supermarket, a dry cleaners, and a bank. Apart from dispensing prescription drugs and selling over-the-counter drugs, Normans' Pharmacy sold candy bars, plastic model-car kits, comic books, *MAD* magazines, and paperback books that were held in a revolving rack. And, there was a soda fountain, with six stools. The "soda jerk" was quite often one of the Normans. Pharmacies were handy for picking up the odd gift, like aftershave for your dad. This pharmacy gave out a free-Coke card, with every prescription. I usually had a pile of these cards, for my friends and me to use. My mother took tranquilizers. We would ride our bikes down to Normans' and have a cherry Coke or a vanilla Coke. Those days are gone. Nowadays, pharmacies are corporation-owned, sterile minimarts. Kids don't ride their bikes to them anymore.

What will it be like when we come to the end of the primrose path and petroleum becomes an obsolete commodity? There is an expression: "You can't sell sand to an Arab." The price of sand, as a commodity in the global economy, could possibly go up. The price of glass might skyrocket, despite the fact that glass is a highly-recyclable commodity. In the future there will be no more petrochemical bottles.

Apparently, the macroeconomists and their cohorts don't care to see the trees for the forest. Individuals, on the other hand, appear to be having difficulty seeing the forest for the trees, from behind the barricade of clutter that has accumulated in their lives. Where do we go from here? Nobody is going to get off scot-free.

Made in the USA
Lexington, KY
09 December 2011